AF540810

EDUCATIONAL PHILOSOPHIC BELIEFS

EDUCATIONAL PHILOSOPHIC BELIEFS

By

Mrs. T. Lalitha
M.A., M.Ed., M.Phil.
Research Scholar
Department of Education
Osmania University
Hyderabad–500 007

Editors

Dr. K.S. Prabhakaran
M.Sc., M.Ed., Ph.D.
Lecturer in Mathematics
M.N.R. College of Education
Ranga Reddy, A.P.

Dr. D.S.N. Sastry
M.Sc., M.Ed., Ph.D.
Reader
A.J. College of Education
Machilipatnam, A.P.

Dr. Digumarti Bhaskara Rao
M.Sc., M.A., M.A., M.Ed., Ph.D.
Reader and Research Director
R.V.R. College of Education
Guntur–522 006

DISCOVERY PUBLISHING HOUSE
NEW DELHI-110002

First Published-2004

Reprinted: 2013

ISBN 81-7141-765-5

Published by

DISCOVERY PUBLISHING HOUSE

4831/24, Ansari Road, Prahlad Street,
Darya Ganj, New Delhi-110002 (India)
Phone: 23279245 • Fax: 91-11-23253475
E-mail:dphtemp@indiatimes.com

Printed at:
Dynamic printers, Delhi

PREFACE

Everyone works satisfactorily, if he/she finds purpose in the work, which forms the purpose or meaning in life.

Educational philosophic beliefs are the beliefs towards education and educational practices.

The present investigation is intended to study the level of meaning in life and educational philosophic beliefs of prospective teachers and the relationship between these two concepts.

The prospective teachers are experiencing loss of meaning in life and are eclectic in educational philosophy. There is no relationship between meaning in life and educational philosophic beliefs.

This book will be of great use to policy planners, teacher educators and educational administrators along with preservice and inservice teachers.

Dr. Digumarti Bhaskara Rao

CONTENTS

INTRODUCTION

One can reach excellence to one's work if one puts his heart in his work. One puts his heart in one's work if one finds that the work is meaningful and the work promotes one's meaning or purpose of life. The meaning that one finds in his life is influenced by the philosophy of life one holds. This has one implication for the teaching profession. The teacher should have the purpose in life and he/she should find teaching as purposeful. The level of meaning that the teacher finds in his life and in his work may depend on the teacher's philosophy of life.

Edith Weiss Kopf and Joelson (1978), while explaining Frankl's concept of meaning, say that our most powerful longing is not the longing for pleasure, as Freud claimed, or for power, as Adler claimed, instead, it is the longing for meaning, i.e., for a goal, for a task, for something or somebody to live for. Frankl says that the person who has a reason for living can endure almost any mode of life, on the other hand the person who fails to see the reason for his life feels frustrated and experiences burnout.

There are investigations to study purpose/meaning in life with reference to teachers. There are also studies which attempted to associate purpose in life and teacher burnout. But this investigator has not come across any study which tried to find out the association between meaning in life and philosophic beliefs of teachers. This investigation is a humble attempt to find out the association between meaning in life and philosophic beliefs of prospective teachers.

The two concepts, meaning in life and philosophic beliefs, are rather complex and fluid. Hence it is felt necessary to discuss them somewhat elaborately as introduction and critical foundation for this investigation. This will also justify the stand taken by the investigator in respect of the two concepts which are interpreted differently by different scholars. This is also helpful in the choice and construction of the tools of this study.

Philosophies of Education— Classification

This investigation deals with the relationship between educational philosophic beliefs of prospective teachers and their meaning of life. Part of the investigative effort concerns the assessment of prospective teachers on their philosophical beliefs. An "Educational Liberalism Conservatism Scale" (E.L.C.S.) has been used by the investigator for this purpose, assuming that the philosophic educational beliefs of people can be conveniently classified into two groups, namely, liberalism and conservatism.

However, in the history of educational philosophy, we come across a number of schools of philosophy. Hence arises the need for justification of the investigator's choice of the classification mentioned above.

Why Different Classifications?

Many writers on the philosophy of education around the globe made attempts to reduce philosophies to a limited number of types, the so-called schools of philosophical thought. It is, indeed, very difficult, though not impossible, to make a classification of philosophies of education. However, we shall discuss the classification of philosophies of education on three dimensions—philosophical, political and sociological. Before attempting this, the classifications attempted by different philosophers is discussed here to have an analytical view of the philosophical educational stand-points in the background of which the selected dimension may finally be justified. Butler gives philosophical thought under four main heads which are naturalism, idealism, realism, and pragmatism. Dupuis attempted two-way classification of philosophies of education of conservatism and liberalism.

One of the more widespread classifications of educational philosophies is based upon the principles which distinguish the various schools of general philosophy. Thus as schools of educational thought, there are to be found realism, idealism, scholasticism, pragmatism and other forms of naturalism (Smith, B.O., 1960).

Though the aforesaid schools one distinctive, there exist still many similarities among them, i.e., even schools of general philosophy are not themselves mutually exclusive. None of these philosophies repudiates progressive education and accepts it outright. This is true of pragmatism, idealism, realism and scholasticism. But

> "differences among educational ideas found in these philosophies of education occasionally appear to be of less consequence than their difference over ideas of knowledge and existence"
>
> *(Smith, B.O., 1960)*

In fact the different nomenclatures given by different educational philosophers are nothing but the traditional schools of general philosophy oriented to particular social or political beliefs which each philosopher believed. Hence, for a thorough understanding of different educational beliefs and for a broad and simplistic classification of such beliefs for assessing the teachers necessitate a brief survey of the general philosophies.

Classification Based on General Philosophies

The main features of the four schools of philosophy, namely, idealism, naturalism, pragmatism and realism one discussed in detail in the following pages.

Idealism

> "Idealism is a philosophical position which adheres to the view that nothing exists as it is an ideal in the mind of man, the mind of Creator, or in a superior supernatural realm."

Idealists, like realists, exhibit wide variations of belief about philosophical and educational questions. Even so, idealists subscribe in one way or another to the view that consistence and correspondence to reality, as they see reality, are the primary criteria of true ideas. To them the chief purpose of education is 'to develop the individual as a finite personality and to do so in such a way as to bring him into harmony with a superior life.' This aim is to be achieved partly through positive expression of the self, partly by use of dialectic methods to develop judgement and reasoning and partly by teaching those skills, knowledge and ways of thinking essential to responsible citizenship.

The general features of idealism are:

1. Spirit and mind constitute reality.
2. Man being spiritual is a superior creation. The supreme aim of life is the 'exaltation of human personality.'
3. Creator is the source of all knowledge and human values. The goal of human life is to realise the universal mind.
4. Ideals or higher values are not made by man. They have their prior existence. The chief aim of human life is 'to realise these values which are truth, goodness and beauty.'

Human life is the grandest work of Creator. The divine within man has to be unfolded and brought to his consciousness through the cultivation of higher values like truth, goodness and beauty. Human race is one. Education should be universal. Education must contribute to preservation and the development of culture enlarging the boundaries of spiritual realm. Hence idealism emphasizes character-building and character-formation. Man must cultivate his inventive and creative powers.

Curriculum must go beyond books and subject matter to include direction, experimental relation with activities. Pestalozzi, Froebel and others have attempted to provide some classroom teaching techniques.

1. Questioning.
2. Discussion.
3. Lecturing.

Self-insight and self-analysis are the main disciplinary factors developed among the pupils. The teacher must be an ideal person. Right and congenial environment set by the teacher will lead the child towards perfection. He is co-worker with Creator in perfecting man. He is the priest of man's spiritual heritage. He is a philosopher, a friend and a guide.

Naturalism

"Naturalism is the philosophical generalization of science, the application of theories of science to the problems of philosophy."

(Gaind and Sharma, 1993)

Naturalism regards:

1. Man as the child of natures;
2. Man himself is the matter and his mind the result of brain function;
3. Nature alone is the entire reality;
4. Reality is comprised of bodies moving in space;.

Ultimately reality is force or energy.

Education should be in strict conformity with the nature of the child. It encourages, formulates and applies natural laws to the educative process. Naturalism is against the autocratic and intellectual presentations which interferes with the spontaneous development of children. Naturalism is instrumental in the development of the concept of "child-centred education".

The main aim of naturalism is self-expression and self-preservation. Naturalistic curriculum is based upon the psychology of child and gives maximum importance to the age and stage of his development. Naturalism regards child as the supreme centre of educational procedures and also believes that child or the human nature is essentially good and pure. In this scheme of education, the teacher's job is to facilitate the process of child's growth as well as learning.

Pragmatism

"It is the attitude of looking away from first things, principles, categories, supposed necessities and looking towards lost things, fruits, consequences and facts."

It is based on the concept of practice or workability of an idea or theory. Pragmatism gives supreme position to action.

Pragmatists believe that no ideal is perennial. Aims are changeable. They grow out of existing situations. Education must cultivate a dynamic and adaptable mind which may, in turn, successfully cope with life situations and problems. Thus the aim of education is more education and education is a life-long process.

Curriculum includes all experiences received by an individual in different spheres. It ought to be synthetic and integral on the principles of utility and natural interests.

There are no fixed methods of teaching. What to teach is more important. The teacher decides the question "How to teach" depending on each teaching learning situation. The famous 'Project Technique' of teaching is the outcome of pragmatic philosophy. Pragmatists' main concern is inner discipline. Children must know to live a democratic life. Morals grow from democratic living. By sharing responsibilities an individual imbibes virtues like toleration and mutual respect.

A teacher must be a practical, trained, efficient person with vision and foresight. He has to create learning situations and stimulate child's activities.

Realism

"Realism asserts that things can exist without their being known at all. It lays emphasis on the independence of object whether human mind knows about it or not."

The realists hold ultimate reality to be the objective world, a world independent of any and all human experience. Experience is a secondary notion, that a subject and an object must exist in reality before an experience can take place between them. The purpose of experiencing is to gain knowledge of what is.

Realism confines itself to the realm of the natural, to the act of knowing, a form of reaction of the organism to a problem situation.

In the realistic view of education, theory and reason play a central role. The accidental interests of children should not determine the direction of education. The student is given a glimpse of higher wisdom.

Logic, grammar and mathematics are to be taught, not only as tools of communication, but also as instruments for the apprehension of reality.

Classification Based on Sociological Perspectives

Some attempts have been made to classify educational philosophies *in terms of themselves*, rather than in terms of general philosophical outlooks. Perhaps the best-known effort along this line is that which uses *attitude towards education and social change* as the major principle of classification. According to this view, there are four schools of educational philosophy—progressivism, essentialism, perennialism and reconstructionism. (Brameld.T., 1971; Smith, B.O., 1960).

Progressivism

> "Progressivism is the educational expression of the liberal road to culture"
>
> *(Brameld.T., 1955)*

Education means the moulding of the native, impulsive behaviour of the human being into meaningful patterns of habit.

> "Education, then, is a continuing process of the reconstruction of experience."
>
> *Wingo, G.M. (1975)*

Good educational aims will be conceived around the needs, native powers, and previous experience of the person to be educated.

The main task of the school is attending and maintaining a high degree of social integration among the various aspects of society. Stress in the school is laid on the study of social problems to plan to solve them.

The child-centred emphasis is revealed in characteristic concern of the progressivist curriculum for rounded, organismic learning—a curriculum that encourages individual initiative, release of feelings, spontaneity of ideas, creative expression. Such a curriculum requires that the teacher knows every student as thoroughly as possible.

Reconstructionism

Brameld (1971), one of the chief architects of reconstructionism, states the reconstructionist orientation as follows:

> "...We may, on the transformative level, envision, and share in the innovation of cultural designs." Conceived, too, that the present culture is no longer adequate, we would subscribe to the educational beliefs and actions of the reconstructionist orientation."

Quoting once again Kneller (1967), the basic principles of reconstructionism can be expressed in the following lines:

1. The main purpose of education is to promote a clearly thought out programme of social reform.
2. Educators must undertake this task without delay.
3. The new social order must be "genuinely democratic."
4. The teacher should persuade his pupils democratically of the validity and urgency of the reconstructionist point of view.
5. The means and ends of education must be refashioned in accordance with the findings of the behavioural sciences.
6. The child, the school and education itself and shaped largely by social and cultural forces.

The conservative attitude was expressed in two schools of thought—perennialism, aristocratic in temper and consciously philosophic, and essentialism; more moderate and down-to-earth in its spirit.

Essentialism

> "...We may, on the transmissive level, consciously and clearly confirm those habits of living and expressions of belief that have hitherto prevailed in modern culture. In education, should

we settle upon this choice, we would identify ourselves with the kind of educational theory and practice that we shall call the *essentialist orientation.*"

(Brameld.T., 1971)

The basic principles of essentialism, given by Kneller, are as follows:

1. Learning necessarily involves hard work and application.
2. The initiative in education should lie with the teacher rather than the pupil.
3. The core of education is the absorption of prescribed subject matter.
4. The school should retain traditional methods of mental discipline.

Perennialism

"...We may, on the restorative level, celebrate the spirit and principles of an earlier, and, for those of such persuasion, a nobler human order. Convinced that the present culture is failing man, we could insist, educationally, upon a resurrection of the premises and proposals of the *perennialist orientation.*"

(Brameld.T., 1971)

It maintains that the basic principles of education are changeless or perennial. Human nature does not alter but remains essentially the same.

According to Kneller (1967), the basic principles are:

1. Human beings everywhere are basically the same; hence, education should be the same for everyone.
2. Since rationality is man's highest attribute, he must use it to direct his instinctual nature in accordance with deliberately chosen ends.
3. Education's task is to adjust men to the truth, which is eternal, rather than to the contemporary world, which is not.

4. Education is not an imitation of life but a preparation for life.

5. The child should be taught certain basic subjects that will acquaint him with the world's permanencies.

6. Education should introduce the pupil to the universal concerns of mankind through the study of the great works of literature, philosophy, history, and science in which they have been expressed.

Classification Based on Socio-Political Perspective

Educational thought is also conceived by some under two broad categories, namely, authoritarian and democratic. Generally, national governments are considered under these two heads in political philosophy. The educational control is not outside the domain of national politics. Hence the political decisions taken on the foundations of political philosophies also influence educational system. Teacher, who is a central figure in the educational organisation, and also a member of the political organisation, may think and act in terms of the more simplistic and also the more familiar types of political philosophies oriented to education.

> "This authoritarianism approach...is essentially typical or traditional idealism, of many schools of realism, and to a surprisingly large extent, of the ostensibly, 'radical' reconstructionist theory of Brameld mentioned above."
>
> *(Hansen, K.H. 1960).*

Democratic philosophy believes in the rights of an individual citizen. Much freedom will be provided to the pupils. It helps in educating the children to think for themselves.

Justification of Liberal-Constructive Dimension

The so-called schools of philosophy emerge from the already existing philosophical theories in the attempt of man to evolve certain values of life, some beliefs which may guide him in carrying out his professional obligations, in adjusting himself to the new environment on the foundations laid by eminent thinkers.

On the other side of the coin, philosophical tendencies which advocate either *statusquo* or extremely careful planning of change are generally grouped under conervatism. It is conventional to call idealistic and realistic beliefs as conservative. The modern off-springs of these conservative schools, namely, essentialism and perennialism are also called conservatives. Thus in a broad sweeping way, from the politico-social angle the multifarious philosophical schools can be patterned into the two broad categories of conservatism and liberalism.

As it has been already mentioned, the modern philosophies are not mutually exclusive. Since most of them are the result of evolution, they carry with them some of the inheritances of the schools of yester years. Keeping in mind this fact, the different philosophies may be diagrammatically presented, adopting and extending the figuratic representation by Brameld. As such the different philosophies may not be viewed as opposite poles but as different views occupying different places on a conservative-liberal continuum.

Conservatism and Liberalism

This investigator has to categorise the sample of prospective teachers on the basis of their philosophic beliefs and find out if there exists any relationship between their educational philosophic beliefs and their meaning of life. For this purpose a tool should be devised to measure the educational philosophic beliefs of prospective teachers. The tool should not be too technical nor should it be complicated. It should be simple and easy to administer. Hence the investigator chose the liberal-conservatism continuum as the basis for measuring prospective teachers for their philosophic beliefs.

Dictionary of Education (Good, C.V. 1959) defines conservatism as

> "The doctrine or point of view that opposes change for the sake of novelty and advocates changes only with caution and upon sufficient evidence of probable improvement, and stresses the importance of preserving values already achieved."

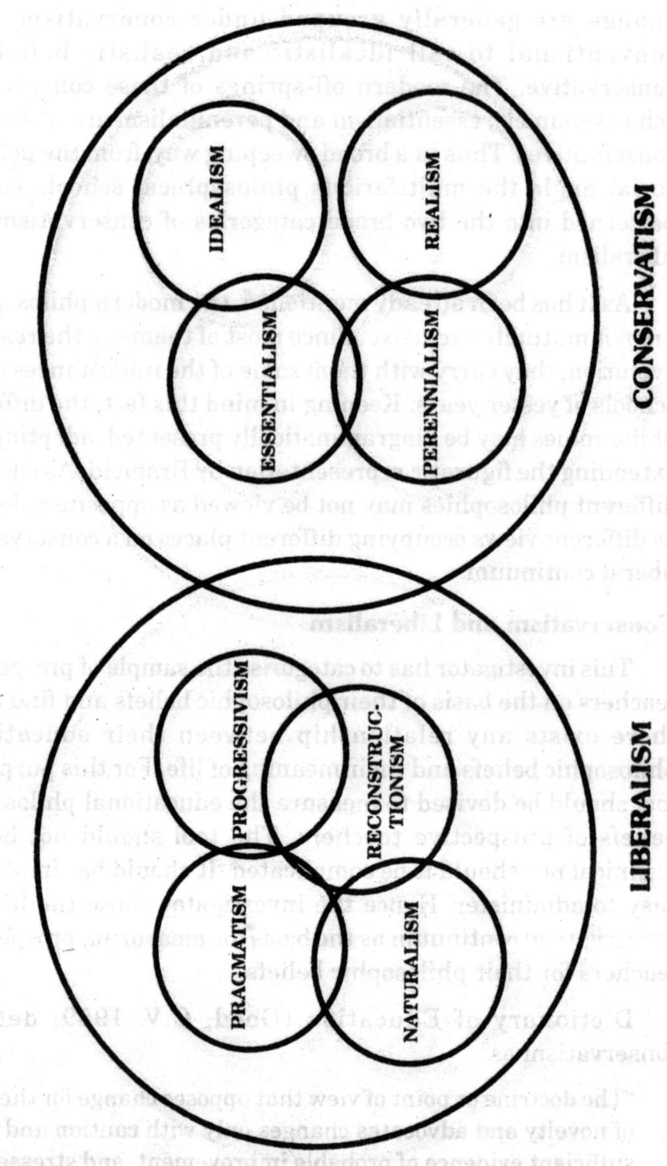
CLASSIFICATION OF PHILOSOPHIES OF EDUCATION-INVESTIGATOR
IDEALISM
REALISM
ESSENTIALISM
PERENNIALISM
CONSERVATISM
PROGRESSIVISM
RECONSTRUC-
TIONISM
PRAGMATISM
NATURALISM
LIBERALISM

The definition of liberalism given by Good (1959) in Dictionary of Education is as follows:

"It is the philosophy of education that advocates freedom of thought and speech and the development of the individual along the lines of his greatest interest and aptitude."

He further defines it as

"the educational philosophy that the mind is liberated through disciplinary studies like those of the classical curriculum, especially logic, mathematics, formal languages and metaphysics."

From the foregoing discussions, the basic tenets of conservatism and liberalism can be summarized here.

Basic tenets of conservatism are:

1. Human nature is everywhere and at all times essentially the same.

2. The main purpose of education should be the same throughout the world. Its purpose is to transmit to the future generation what is conserved in the established traditions of human race.

3. This position emphasizes subject matter and methodology what has been tested by time.

4. There is a strong inclination to view education as only intellectual, and to restrict the scope of the school to "learning tasks."

5. Schools should concentrate on teaching basic skills—such as reading, writing, and mathematics—and leave the problem of personal adjustment, of moral and character development, of citizenship to other agencies in the community and to the family.

6. Education is a discipline, that learning itself trains the individual in responsibility and control.

7. Children should learn to obey and be respectful of authority.

8. The conservative sees value in greater school discipline.

9. Pupil is a Child of creator.
10. Ideas constitute the important content of education.
11. All school activities which are not directly related to subject matter are labelled as "extra-curricular."
12. The methods used should be teacher-centred.
13. Classroom discipline should be very rigorous.
14. The primary objective of evaluation is "to what extent has the student mastered the subject?"
15. Teachers and administrators must abandon the practice of continuous promotion and insist that the students master the subject matter and intellectual skills of each grade before they are promoted.
16. Individual differences need not be stressed since "all human beings" are 'human beings.'

(Dupuis, 1972)

Basic tenets liberalism are:

1. Pupil is a child of nature.
2. The development of the whole child or the development of the person is the main purpose of the school.
3. The chief purpose of education is to enable the child to learn the art of bridging the past and the future based on his present experiences.
4. All activities which take place under the direction and control of the school are integral elements of curriculum.
5. Emphasis should be placed on pupil activity during the class period.
6. The primary objective of evaluation is "to assess a pupil's growth in all phases of living."
7. Individual differences should be stressed.
8. There are no absolute norms or standards based on the mastery of any given content.

9. Sports, social functions, club activities, crafts and the like one worthy components of the curriculum.

10. The teacher should make the class well disciplined with the cooperative efforts of the partners engaged in learning activities.

11. Man is not everywhere and at all times essentially the same.

(Dupuis, 1972)

From the statements of the liberal and conservative positions given above, it can be seen that the two are a kind of eclectic philosophies instead of pure and unmixed schools. In a way the two positions explain the two broad attitudes of a person towards education and educational practices. Thus standing as today a teacher can be said to be a conservative or a liberal sooner than to be an idealist or a pragmatist. Hence this investigator is justified in categorizing prospective teachers into two broad groups, namely, conservatives and liberals on the basis of their educational philosophic beliefs. It is necessary for this investigation to identify liberal and conservative prospective teachers in order to find out if there is any relation between the philosophic beliefs of prospective teachers and their meaning in life. This investigator adopted the Educational Liberalism-Conservatism Scale (E.L.C.S.) developed earlier by Sastry (1980).

This tool consists of ninety-one statements of educational beliefs associated with conservative and liberal philosophies.

Meaning in Life

The meaning in life must be conceived in terms of the specific meaning of a personal life in a given situation. Life is a chain of questions which man has to answer by being responsible, by making decisions. Each question has only one answer, the right one. This does not imply that man is always capable of finding the right answer or solution to each problem, of finding the true meaning to his existence. As a finite being he is not exempt from error but he has to try to reach the absolute rest.

Man is guided in search for meaning by his conscience, the intuitive capacity of man to find out the meaning of a situation. It follows that psychotherapist must not impose a value on the patient who must be referred to his own conscience. Logo therapy only acts as a catalyst to start the individual's own wheels of self-analysis turning once again.

According to Frankl, life can be made meaningful through three value areas—creative, experimental and attitudinal. First, through what we give to life, in terms of our creations and achievements. Second, by what we take from the world in terms of our experiences and encounters e.g. by experiencing truth, goodness and beauty, by experiencing nature and culture, by encountering and loving another human being. Third, through the attitude or stand we take toward life, toward a fate we can no longer change, toward. What Frankl calls 'tragic triad' of human existence made up of pain, guilt and death.

Logo therapy teaches that there are no tragic and negative aspects which cannot be, by the stand one takes to them, transmuted in to positive accomplishments. In the case of pain one takes a stand toward one's fate which cannot be changed but in the case of guilt one takes a stand to one's self as man may well change himself. The third aspect, life's transitoriness, adds to man's responsibilities, for he is all the more responsible for using the passing opportunities to actualise potentialities, to realize values, to make life meaningful.

However, conditions may vary in the degree to which they make it easier or more difficult for an individual to find meaning in his life or to fulfil the meaning of a given situation. We can consider the different societies and the different extents to which they promote or inhibit meaning fulfilment. In principle, nevertheless, the fact remains that meaning is available under any conditions, even the worst conceivable ones.

Conceptual Framework-Relation Between Meaning in Life and Educational Philosophic Beliefs:

1. Meaning in life is key concept used by the followers of logo therapy while interpreting the emotional state of their clients. According to Frankl, every individual

seeks the meaning of life. The result of the search is influenced by the human and societal situation. These two situations threaten the individual. The meaning which one finds depends on his response to the threats. Many followers of logo therapy believe that during 1970's most of the American youths failed to respond satisfactorily to these threats. They fail to find meaning in their life, they experienced meaning in their life, they experienced meaninglessness at different levels. Crumbaugh's 'Purpose in Life Scale' (P.I.L. Scale) is designed to measure the level of meaninglessness experiences by the client.

In this background Indians may be curious to know what is the general experience of Indian youth today because, the trends of post-modern society felt in America during 1960 and 1970's are now present in the Indian society.

2. It is the presumption of the investigator that individuals in a particular society hold certain beliefs about man and his relationship to the environment. These beliefs may be identified as liberal, conservative out-look to life. This philosophical position influences the person's attitude towards death, pain and such universal experiences which the logo-therapy call the human situations as also the individual's attitude to work, fun and such other experiences which they call the societal situation.

3. The person with conservative philosophical beliefs is not easily open to multiple options in a choice situation and if he is hesitant, he/she is likely to experience frustration, and hopelessness in the face of societal and human threats. In terms of existential—phenomenological philosophy this person experiences lack of meaning in life or loss of purpose in life. Such persons, therefore, score high when measured on P.I.L. On the other hand the person who is on the liberal side of philosophical beliefs tends to score low on P.I.L. Because he/she is not deterministic, he/she does not

find options closed. Such persons are not easily frustrated in their search for meaning in their work and in their life.

4. Teacher trainees are in their youth like the American youths. Indian prospective teachers may also experience existential vacuum. A nation needs teachers who emotionally involve in their profession (work). This happens when the prospective teachers join the profession, with a purpose and meaning in their work. If we can find that their educational beliefs have an association with the experienced level of meaning, it will be easier to identify effective teachers.

It is in this background this investigator wants to find out if there is any association between the educational philosophic beliefs of prospective teachers and their levels of meaning of life/purpose in life and if there exists an association, what is the nature of the association.

STATEMENT OF THE PROBLEM

"A study of the meaning in life of prospective teachers in relation to their educational philosophic beliefs."

Objectives of the Study

1. To find out if the levels of meaning in life held by the prospective teachers have any relation to their philosophic beliefs in terms of conservative-liberal continuum.

2. To find out if the M.I.L.-philosophic belief relationship exists differently in men and women prospective teachers.

3. To find out if sex makes any difference in the scores obtained by the prospective teachers on the P.I.L. scale.

4. To find out if the subjects of study at graduation makes any difference in the scores obtained by the prospective teachers on the P.I.L. scale.

5. To find out if sex makes any difference in the philosophic beliefs of prospective teachers.

6. To find out if the different subjects of study in the basic degree by the prospective teachers makes any difference in their philosophic beliefs.

Hypotheses of the Study

1. Meaning in life held by prospective teachers has relationship with their philosophic beliefs.
2. The correlation value of M.I.L. and educational philosophic beliefs for men significantly differs from that for women.
3. There is a positive correlation between Li-Co ratios and P.I.L. scores of liberals on E.L.C.S.
4. Prospective teachers who are conservative on the Li-Co ratios scale score low on the P.I.L. scale.
5. Sex makes a difference in the level of experience of purpose in life.
6. Sex makes a difference in the expressed educational philosophic beliefs.
7. The means scores on P.I.L. scale obtained by prospective teachers with mathematics, biological sciences and social sciences background differ significantly.
8. Mathematics, biological sciences and social science teacher trainees differ in their educational philosophic beliefs.

DEFINITIONS OF THE KEY TERMS

Belief

Steiner and Fishbein (1965) defines

"belief is a unidimensional concept which refers only to the probability or improbability of the existence of a partial object or a particular relationship towards the object,"

According to Krech and Crutch Field (1948)

"A belief is an enduring organisation of perceptions and cognitions about some aspect of individual world."

In the words of Hunt (1975).
"belief is an intellectual assent or anything which a person regards as true."

The word does connote conviction, for example, a religious belief, but to limit belief to this nongeneric usage virtually demands the frequent use of some substitute and makes writing unnecessarily complicated. The present study conforms to the definition given by Hunt (1975).

Educational Philosophic Beliefs

In this work educational philosophic beliefs stand for the conservative or liberal beliefs of an individual related to education and educational practices.

Meaning in Life

Meaning in life refers to the perceived meaning in life expressed by an individual when measured on P.I.L. scale which was developed by Crumbaugh based on the concept of Frankl's concept of meaning in life. This concept is the result of the application of the existential philosophy to psychotherapy.

P.I.L. Scale

This abbreviation is for purpose in life scale wherever it occurs in this report.

Limitations of the Study

1. For testing the association between P.I.L. and educational philosophic beliefs of prospective teachers the study is limited to the extreme groups of the educational liberalism-conservatism continuum.

2. The level of significance considered is 0.05.

REVIEW OF RELATED RESEARCH

In the present study, a review of related research has yielded very rich dividends. It was possible for the research to delimit and define the present problem on the basis of the researches undertaken earlier. Above all, the reviews gave very clear insight into the study area, enabling the researcher to define the objectives, the scope, measurement, and methodology. It was also possible to plan a new venture resulting in new relationships. Keeping in view what has already been accomplished in earlier researches, adequate care was taken to avoid duplication of established findings. Suitable extensions and modifications were made to prosecute new avenues of scope and procedure.

Educational philosophy of teachers plays an important role in determining their classroom behaviour. Teachers' educational philosophy determines the success of education.

It is surprising to note that though the study of educational philosophy of teachers is of great importance, very few attempts have been made so for at various levels.

Research Studies on Meaning in Life

The relationship between meaninglessness or scores on the low end of the continuum of the purpose in life test and unsuccessful living has been validated in studies that have shown strong relationship between low purpose/meaning in life scores and deviant behaviour such as psychiatric disorder, delinquency, drug addiction and alcoholism. Psychiatric populations tend to score significantly lower on the meaning in life than non-patient population (Crumbaugh and Maholick, 1964, 1969; Yarnell, 1971). Pearson and Shaffield (1974) in a study of 144 British neurotic out-patients with the purpose/meaning in life test and the eyesenck personality inventory (Form-A) found that highly neurotic and socially introverted patients had lower purpose/meaning in life score.

Famiiletti (1975) noted that delinquent high school boys scored significantly lower on the purpose/meaning in life than non-delinquent boys. Among adults, Black and Gregson (1973) reported that recidivists scored significantly lower than did first-time offenders On the other hand, normals scored significantly higher than both first-time offenders and recidivists.

Shen and Fechtman (1971) found significantly lower purpose/meaning in life scores among college students who were regular users of marijuana as compared to non-drug users. Likewise, Padleford (1974) studied high school students and discovered that students with low scores on purpose/meaning in life had significantly higher level of drug involvement than those who scored high in purpose/meaning in life. Parallel findings have been reported with alcoholism.

The other end of the continuum in the P.I.L. scores is represented by meaningfulness and it is Frankl's contention that this concept is a reliable criterion of mental health.

Kotchen (1960) found a significant positive correlation between meaning orientation and mental health, the criteria of which were responsibility, uniqueness, courage, self affirmation faith-commitment, transcendent and world view.

Crumbaugh (1968) also found the highest P.I.L. scores among well motivated and successful professional and business population.

Crumbaugh, *et.al.* (1970) found that a high degree of purpose/meaning in life is both possessed and needed for success in a religious order.

Crandal and Rasmussen's (1975) study, on the relationship between P.I.L. and values in college students revealed that

(a) low score on the P.I.L. were associated with the values of pleasure, excitement and comfort, supporting Frankl's contention that a humanistic approach to life tends to be self-defeating and tends to promote an existential vacuum;

(b) high scores on the P.I.L. was associated with the value of salvation, confirming the results of Crumbaugh *et.al.* (1970);

(c) P.I.L. scores were found to correlate highly with intrinsic religious orientation and not with extrinsic orientation, suggesting that a genuine intrinsic religious orientation helps to foster greater meaning of life, even among normal range of lay people.

Butler and Carr (1968) studied the relationship between meaning in life and social action and found the more socially active students scoring higher on the P.I.L. but the differences were not significant.

Rude (1981) found that male adolescents with low P.I.L. scores differed significantly from their peers in beliefs of capacity, opportunity and identification and they also had significantly lower positive peer ratings.

In relation to P.I.L. and sex, the evidence is inconclusive. Butler and Carr (1968), Doerries (1970) and Pedleford (1974) found that females scored higher on P.I.L. than males. In contrast, Pearson and Shefield (1975) reported that males scored higher on P.I.L. than females. However most of the research has indicated no significant difference between males and females (Crumbaugh and Maholick, 1964; Meir and Edwards, 1974; Jacobson and Ritter, 1977).

No substantial relationships are reported between the P.I.L. and educational level (Crumbaugh and Maholik 1964), intelligence (Yarnell, 1971). However, Butler and Carr (1968) found that Blacks scored significantly higher than Whites; whereas Padelford (1974) reported that Blacks and Mexican Americans had lower scores than Whites.

Sultana (1983) studied the effect of purpose/meaning in life on adjustment of adolescents in Bangladesh and found the following results:

(a) *Effect of purpose / meaning in life on Home adjustment:* High P.I.L. group had least adjustment problems whereas low P.I.L. group had considerably high rate of adjustment problems.

(b) *Effect of purpose / meaning in life on health adjustment:* The results shows that the higher the meaning in life scores, lesser was the adjustment problems. Except the high P.I.L. group within each P.I.L. group, girls seem to be better adjusted to their health than boys. In the high P.I.L. group adolescent boys seem to experience less adjustment problems related to their health than the adolescent girls.

(c) *Effect of purpose / meaning in life on social adjustment:* Results indicated that higher P.I.L. groups were socially better adjusted than the lower P.I.L. groups. With in each P.I.L. group, adolescent boys experienced less problems in their social adjustment than adolescent girls.

(d) *Effect of purpose / meaning in life on emotional adjustment.* Results suggested that adolescents with higher P.I.L. were comparatively better adjusted to their emotion than adolescents with lower P.I.L.

(e) *Effect of purpose / meaning in life on educational adjustment:* Significant difference between different P.I.L. groups indicate that Bangladesh adolescents with higher P.I.L. were better adjusted to their education than adolescents with lower P.I.L.

(f) *Effect of purpose / meaning in life on total adjustment:* Results suggest that Bangladesh adolescents with high P.I.L. were overall better adjusted than the other P.I.L. groups. A high P.I.L. makes the person oriented toward actualisation of his creative, experimental and attitudinal values.

In a comparative study of four equally distributed disabled and non-disabled groups of 100 Indian samples, Gon and Mehta (1982) found a trend toward high P.I.L. All four groups differed significantly on item analysis of P.I.L. But no significant difference was found in P.I.L. among both the sexes.

In an other investigation on an Indian sample, Gonsalvez and Gon (1983) studied the degree and pattern of meaning in life (P.I.L.). The sample consisted of four psychopathological normal groups. Their findings show that each of the psychopathological groups experienced a significantly lower degree of meaning in life (P.I.L.) than each of the normal population.

Mohanty, R.K. (1990) made a study of meaning in life, burnoutness and work orientation of teacher educators of Orissa. Major findings of the study with regard to meaning in life are as follows:

1. The level of meaning in life of the sample in the present study as measured by purpose in life test is low—the mean = 97.39 is lower than the mean P.I.L. scores of normal populations of other available studies range from 110.03 (Yarnel, 1971) to 119.00 (Crumbaugh and Maholick, 1964) and also lower than the mean P.I.L. of Calcutta teachers. (Mean = 100.86, Misra, 1986).
2. The study shows that the teacher educators high in meaning in life are working with achievement orientation and teacher educators low in meaning in life are working with affiliation orientation.

STUDIES ON EDUCATION PHILOSOPHIC BELIEFS

A brief review of the previous studies and investigations pertaining to the educational philosophic beliefs of prospective teachers is of immense value to know the need for the present study and also to decide the nature of the study.

Educational philosophy of teacher plays an important role in determining their classroom behaviour. Teacher's educational philosophy determines the success of education. It is surprising to note that though the study of educational philosophy of teachers is of great importance, very few attempts have been made so far at various levels.

Problems of education and of philosophy one interrelated. Proper understanding of the problems in education can be had if the philosophy behind that particular system of education is well understood. Surprisingly, though many investigations into the problems in education and of teachers have been undertaken, only few attempts towards the study of philosophy of education have been made. A brief review of the previous studies relating to educational philosophy are given under.

Oliver and Butcher (1962) investigated whether or not teacher's attitudes toward education might be represented by the dimension of naturalism, radicalism, and tender mindedness. A factor analysis of data collected on 300 teachers provided support for the existence of three distinct categories of teacher's attitudes and beliefs.

Kerlinger and Kaya (1959) found "progressivism and traditionalism" to be two relatively independent and orthogonal attitudinal dimensions, a result which appears to contradict the common sense notion that they are opposite poles of a single continuum. In a later study, using an expanded collection of items, Kerlinger (1967) found eight correlated first-order factors, and two second-order factors. He called the first second factor, which emphasized strict discipline, subject matter, and moral standards, as traditionalism; while the second order factor, which stressed child needs, individual differences and social learning was labeled progressivism. As Kerlinger has observed, common sense would suggest that persons holding progressive attitude toward education would tend to disagree with traditional ideas, while those with traditional views would look with disfavour or progressivism.

Miller (1963) from Washington State University made an investigation into the "educator's attitudes toward educational practices." The purpose of the study is to determines whether there are differences of attitudes in regard to educational procedures. The main object has been to test specifically the differences of attitudes within the profession between various sub-groups.

The attitudes taken by the investigator are:

1. Child-centred education favourable
2. Chile-centred education unfavourable
3. Subject-centred education favourable
4. Subject-centred education unfavourable
5. School-community cooperation favourable
6. School-community cooperation unfavourable

Variables like geographical location, subjects handling and the kind of job held are considered. Questionnaire was constructed exemplifying the aforesaid attitudes and respondents were asked to indicate agreement or disagreement. Responses of the groups were compared by the Chi-Square.

Finally, through his study, the investigator concluded that the responding educators distinguished between favourable and unfavourable attitudes also concluded that the attitudes of teachers differ viewing various educational practices.

Jain investigated into 'the philosophy of teacher education as held by some of teacher educators in U.P. and Delhi." Subjects considered were teachers of training colleges, for secondary school teachers.

The investigator adopted the questionnaire technique supported by interview. Variables like experience and qualification were considered. Skills and qualities required of a teacher, student teacher relationship, limitations of the present programme of teacher education, methods of teaching and the extent to which freedom to children be given were taken as the areas of study.

Through this investigation, the investigator concluded that the philosophy of teacher education held by some teacher educators in "eclectic."

Pramod Kumar (1978) made an investigation of the "comparative study of educational attitudes." The subjects for this study are student-teachers and in-service teachers. The investigator adopted the educational attitude inventory originally developed by Heng and Chong. This inventory includes four dimensions of attitudes towards teaching, namely, attitude towards child; attitudes towards discipline; attitude towards methods; and attitudes towards administration. Variables like academic qualifications, teaching experience, and sex were considered. The investigator arrived at the following conclusions:

1. Science teachers have favourable attitude towards discipline as compared to non-science teachers in general.
2. Post-graduate teachers have favourable attitudes towards administration when compared with graduate teachers.
3. Teaching experience has little relation with attitudes.
4. Female teachers have favourable educational attitude than male teachers. In addition, female teachers have favourable attitude towards discipline and administration as compared to male teachers.

Some of the previous investigations discussed above obviously, do not make an attempt to study the teacher's beliefs according to the principles of generally accepted schools of philosophy, such as naturalism, idealism, realism and pragmatism and the broad aspects of education as viewed by them.

However, the study of Miller (1963) reveals the fact that the attitudes of teachers towards educational practices differ due to the differences in their philosophies of education. Philosophy of education of the teachers is thus found to be influencing their view of educational practices.

With this view, Jagannadharao (1971) made an attempt of "A critical study of the educational philosophy of teachers working in secondary schools."

He adopted the questionnaire technique. Variables like experience, sex and residence were considered. Aims and purpose of education; curriculum; methodology; role of teacher; discipline and behavioural change were taken as the areas of study under each school of philosophy, namely, naturalism, idealism, realism and pragmatism.

Through this investigation, the investigator concluded that teachers have a liking for pragmatic, idealistic and realistic schools and philosophy and there is no appreciation of naturalistic philosophy. The have no belief exclusively in a single school of philosophy. Different aspects of different schools of philosophy are believed. From this study, it is obvious that there is an eclectic tendency among teachers.

Victor (1976) attempted to study "The relation between teacher belief and teacher personality in four samples of teacher trainees." The investigator tried to *(a)* examine the interdependence among the Wehling and Charters dimensions (subject matter emphasis; personal adjustment ideology; student autonomy vs. teacher direction; emotional disengagement; consideration of student view-points; classroom order; student challenge and integrative learning; *(b)* study relationships of these dimensions of belief to conceptual level, dogmatism, field independence and self-disclosure and *(c)* examine the consistency of the findings to clarify the multidimensional nature of the beliefs. The following results were reported:

1. Three factors combining teacher beliefs and personality variables were consistently formed over samples.
2. Factor I was always a teacher-centeredness factor with emotional disengagement, dogmatism, subject matter emphasis.
3. Factor II was student concern factor with personal adjustment ideology, consideration of students' view-points and integrative learning.
4. Factor III was autonomy-control with teacher direction and conceptual level.
5. Field independence was typically a specific factor and does not illustrate consistent conservation with any of the variables represented in these samples.
6. The present findings gave general support for a multi-dimensional view of teacher beliefs and personality similar to Wehling and Charters. With the present data identifying three broad areas of relation between teacher beliefs and teacher personality.

Oliveer (1970) studied the problem of education lag as represented by a study of the stated educational beliefs of teachers as contrasted to their classroom practices. The study was geared to four universally accepted principles of learning. The selected principles were as follows:

1. Good teaching recognizes and provides for individual differences among children.
2. Human growth and development is a continuous process.
3. Real learning is based upon experiencing.
4. Learning proceeds best when related to the interests and experiences of the learner.

One hundred nineteen teachers representing all grade levels from kindergarten through the eighth grade were selected for the study. A fifty-item checklist of educational beliefs was prepared. The respondents indicated their acceptance or rejection of these statements by checking their response as "agree" or "disagree."

The second phase of the study was concerned with the evaluation of the classroom practices of these teachers as reflected in the learning situations in their classrooms. For this purpose, a suitable evaluative device was prepared.

The investigator reported that there is little relationship between the professed educational beliefs of the teachers and their classroom practices. The correlation between the belief scores and the evaluative scores was 0.31, an extremely low correlation indicating practically no relationship.

Sastry (1980) made a study of the classroom behaviour of teachers in relation to their philosophic beliefs in education. Some major findings are as follows:

1. There is no significant relationship between the stated educational philosophic beliefs and classroom behaviour of teachers.
2. None of the following variables makes any difference for the relationship between educational philosophic beliefs and classroom behaviour of teachers.

(a) Sex

(b) Age

(c) Teaching experience

(d) Professional qualifications

(e) Professional status

(f) Location of the school.

In the fifth Survey of Educational Research (1988-92), Vol. I. Dr. Seshadri in his trend report on 'Philosophy of Education' makes a mention that the 38 studies classified as philosophy of education research include studies of different types and foci. The bag also includes a few studies which are of the survey and historical research types and a couple of research articles.

The dominating category, as usual, is the study of the educational philosophy/contributions of individual thinkers, philosophy schools, scriptures, historical/cultural periods. Nearly 70 per cent of the researches (26) account for this type. Some of these (7) are studies that are set in a comparative frame researches that focus on philosophy/educational themes account for the remaining.

Dr. Seshadri concludes his trend report by saying that sadly philosophy of educational research continues to be imprisoned in the constricting paradigm of study of the past.

None of these studies includes the educational philosophic beliefs of teachers/teacher trainees of the present day.

3

RESEARCH PROCEDURE

Instrumentation

This study requires the measurement of purpose in life (P.I.L.) and educational philosophic beliefs on the sample. For this, tools to measure P.I.L. and educational philosophic beliefs are required. To measure P.I.L. of prospective teachers, the purpose in life test by Crumbaugh and Maholick (1969) was selected as an instrument to measure Viktor Frankl's concept in meaning in life. The reason for the selection of this test was that it was specifically designed to measure Frankl's concepts of existential vacuum and noogenic neurosis and it has been widely used for measuring the concept of meaning in life.

In addition, it has been validated against Frankl's questionnaire, the series of questions which Frankl developed to measure existential vacuum. Also this tool was used in Indian conditions by Monica Misra (1986), Mohanty (1990) etc Hence this tool was selected to measure meaning in life of prospective teachers.

Purpose in Life Scale

The P.I.L. test consists of three parts. Part A has 20 scaled Likert type sentence stems each with 7 response alternatives ranging from 1 (low purpose) to 7 (high purpose). Descriptive terms are used as anchors for the extreme points 1 and 7 and position No. 4 is considered neutral.

For example:

I usually am

1	2	3	4	5	6	7
Completely bored			Neutral			Exuberant enthusiastic

Part B has 13 sentence completion items and part C requires writing of a paragraph on personal aims, ambitions and goals. Part A is the only one which is treated quantitatively and has been the subject of most research efforts to date. Part B and C are not scored and little consideration is given to them in either the manual or published research (Braun, 1972; Domino, 1972). The present study has utilized Part A of the instrument, the only part that has been validated.

Educational Philosophic Beliefs Scale

To assess the educational philosophic beliefs of prospective teachers, the investigator made use of *Educational Liberalism-Conservatism Scale* (E.L.C.S.), prepared and validated by Sastry (1980). The original tool consists of eight dimensions containing ninety-one times, out of which 49 items come under liberal philosophy of education and the remaining under conservative philosophy of education. The eight dimensions are:

1. Nature of human being
2. Aims of education
3. Purpose of the school
4. Curriculum
5. Methodology
6. Freedom and discipline
7. Evaluation
8. Truth and good

For the present study only six dimensions are selected containing fifty-six items, out of which twenty-nine items are liberal and twenty-seven items are conservative. Against each of the statements two columns are provided under the captions A and D. A stands for the agreement with the statement and D stands for the disagreement with the statement. Otherwise the scale is constructed on a 'two-point scale.' The teacher trainees are asked to tick in the appropriate column. The scale is presented in the 'closed' form. Copy of the tool was presented in appendix A. The split up of these items under various dimensions of the two philosophies of education are presented in Table—3.1.

Table—3.1 Split up of times—educational liberalism—conservatism scale

S.No.	*Dimension*	*Liberal*	*Conservative*	*Total*
1.	Aims of education	4	4	8
2.	Purpose of school	3	3	6
3.	Curriculum	6	6	12
4.	Methodology	8	6	14
5.	Freedom and discipline	5	5	10
6.	Evaluation	3	3	6
	Total	**29**	**27**	**56**

Selection of the Sample

There are six universities which have affiliated colleges of education in Andhra Pradesh. The investigator decided to select one university area to take up the study. For this the random sampling technique was used. Six slips containing numbers 1 to 6 separately are placed in a box and shuffled. One slip was taken up. Thus Nagarjuna University was selected for this study. The geographical jurisdiction of Nagarjuna University covers Kirshna district, Guntur district and Prakasam district. Nine colleges of education are situated in these three districts. The investigator applied random sampling technique to select one of these three districts by following the above mentioned procedure. Krishna district was thus selected.

In Krishna district, there are four colleges of education with a total intakes of 720.

Administration of the Tool

The investigator approached the principals and took their permission to administer the tools to the prospective teachers. Though the total intake capacity is 720, the investigator followed random sampling technique to select the sample. The nominal rolls were collected from each college of education and candidates with odd numbered roll numbers were chosen, after following the above-mentioned procedure of random selection. Thus three hundred and sixty (360) prospective teachers were chosen for final administration of the test. The total 20 teacher trainees were absent on the test days from all the four colleges of education. Hence 340 teacher trainees took the tools. At the time of verification, before processing the data, it was found that ten teacher trainees did not respond to too many items of the two tools. These ten teacher trainees were not considered for the statistical treatment of the data.

Therefore, the response sheets of the remaining 330 were processed. The description of the sample is presented in Table—3.2.

Table—3.2 Description of the sample—variable-wise

S.No.	*Variable*	*Size*	*Total*
1.	*Sex*		
	A– Men	168	
	B– Women	162	330
2.	*Methodology subject*		
	Mathematics	171	
	Biological science	104	
	Social studies	55	330

Scoring Procedure

A. The P.I.L. is a non-timed self-administering attitude scale and the total score is the sum of the numerical values circled for the twenty items, therefore, the score can theoretically range from 20 to 140. The direction of the magnitude was randomized for the items so that position preference could be minimized (Crumbaugh and Maholick, 1964).

B. Only agreed items of each philosophy of education were considered separately. Thus all the responses of the teacher trainees were tabulated. For each trainee, the proportion of agreed items under each philosophy of education were calculated. By using the following formula, *Liberalism-Conservatism Ratio.*

(Li-Co Ratio) was computed for each individual trainee.

LI-CO Ratio =

Proportion of agreed items under liberal philosophy of education ÷ proportion of agreed items under conservative philosophy of education.

Computation of Li-Co Ratio: Example:

The responses of a teacher trainee were as follows.

Agreed items under liberal philosophy of education = 24. Proportion of agreed items under liberal philosophy of education = 24/29

Agreed items under conservative philosophy of education = 18 proportion of agreed items under conservative philosophy of education = 18/27

Therefore, Li-Co Ratio =

$$\frac{24}{29} \times \frac{27}{18} = 1.24$$

The Li-Ratio of this teacher trainee was 1.24

Thus the responses of all the three hundred and thirty teacher trainees were converted into Li-Co Ratios. These ratios were tabulated and appropriate statistical techniques (mean and standard deviations) were calculated.

Statistical Techniques Adopted

Product moment coefficient of correlation was calculated for the data P.I.L. scores and Li-Co Ratios. Means and standard deviations were computed for Li-Co Ratios and P.I.L. scores separately and critical ratio was computed to test the significant difference between men and women prospective teachers. ANOVA was adopted to test the significant difference among the three groups (mathematics, biological, sciences and social studies) for P.I.L. scores and Li-Co Ratio separately. Appropriate statistical technique used to test each of the seven hypotheses formulated is presented in Table—3.3.

Table—3.3 Hypothesis—Appropriate statistical technique

S.No.	*Hypothesis*	*Statistical technique*
1.	H_1	Product moment coefficient of correlation and chi-square
2.	H_2	Product moment coefficient of correlation and critical ratio
3.	H_3	Product moment coefficient of correlation
4.	H_4	Product moment coefficient of correlation
5.	H_5	Critical ratio
6.	H_6	Critical ratio
7.	H_7	ANOVA
8.	H_7	ANOVA

ANALYSIS OF DATA AND INTERPRETATION OF RESULTS

The purpose of this investigation is to describe the sample prospective teachers of Krishna district in terms of purpose in life and educational philosophic beliefs. It is also proposed to understand the association between purpose in life and educational philosophic beliefs held by the sample population. To obtain the basic data two tools have been selected. They are:

1. P.I.L. scale developed by Crumbaugh and Maholick
2. Educational liberalism conservatism scale developed by Sastry.

The two tools were administered to 330 prospective teachers in four colleges of education located in Krishna district in Andhra Pradesh. While selecting the sample, care has been taken to cover the sex and subjects of study variables (methodology subjects). Details of variable-wise distribution of the sample has been given in Chapter—3.

Means and standard deviations for the two sets of scores obtained with the sample population on the two groups have been computed. They are further subjected to appropriate statistical treatment for purpose of analysis of the data. The results of the analysis of the consequent data are reported in the following pages.

Nature of the Sample in Terms of Meaning in Life

It is to be recalled that the P.I.L. scale was constructed on the basis of the concept of meaning in life. Many previous investigations concerned with meaning in life used P.I.L. scale to measure the level of meaning of life of the given samples (Doeries—1970; Rasmussen—1975; Mehta—1982, and Misra—1986). In this dissertation also the P.I.L. scores are interpreted in terms of meaning of life.

The following are the basic data obtained from the administration of the P.I.L. to the sample prospective teachers.

Sample population	=	330
Scale range	=	20-140
Obtained range	=	58-133
Standard deviation (S.D.)	=	16.37
Mean of men	=	99-53
Men of women	=	98.98

Scores obtained by a group or an individual in psychological measurement cannot help us in understanding in group or individual's status directly. Interpretation of the scores can only be relative. The scores of the group or the individual will get meaning only with reference to norms of the tools if available in comparison with the performance of other groups or individuals on the same tool or related tools. The P.I.L. data given above therefore can better be interpreted in comparison with the results obtained in other studies with the P.I.L. test. In Table—4.1 the mean P.I.L. scores obtained in the present investigation are compared with the P.I.L. means reported in other studies conducted in India and abroad.

Among the available mean scores as reported in Table—4.1 the Deoris groups are the only ones with which the group of the present study can be appropriately compared because of similarity of age and work world. The mean scores of the prospective teachers in the present study which is 99.41 nearly equals the mean score of low participating college students However, the high participating college students are higher in

Table—4.1 Comparison of mean P.I.L. scores

Study	*Nature of sample*	*Mean*
Studies abroad		
Crumbaugh and Maholick (1964)	Non patients	119.00
Crumbaugh and Maholick (1968)	Normal group	112.42
Doeris (1970)	Low participating students	100.45
	High participating students	106.10
Crandal and Rasmussen (1975)	Not known	108.89
Ruffin (1982)	Not known	113.05
Indian studies		
Mehta (1982)	Non handicapped youth	113.64
Misra (1986)	Teachers of Calcutta	100.86
Mohanty (1990)	Teachers educators of Orissa	97.39
Present study	Teacher trainees (Prospective teachers)	99.41

meaning in life with a mean of 106.10. If we consider that all normal adults should be moderate or high, in meaning in life,which is 100.45 (Deoris). then there is meaning in comparing the sample group of the present study with other sample groups. In that case the prospective teachers in this study are low in meaning in life (Mean 99.41) compared to the groups in all foreign studies (Means ranging from 106.45 - 119. However, the prospective teachers of the present study are all most equal in their level of meaning in life with Calcutta teachers and Orissa teacher educators. Existential vacuum or loss of meaning in life will be reflected in the low score on P.I.L. Existential vacuum is regarded as a reflection of the affluent society of the West and should be pronounced among the Western samples. But the available data shows that all the normal Western samples were higher, compared to Indian samples. According to Frankl existential vacuum is associated with loss of traditional values and familial relationships in modern Western society. Indians because of their strong traditional values and familial support until late in adulthood are expected to experience less degree of existential anxiety and scores higher on P.I.L. when compared to their Western counterparts. In this connection, Mohanty feels that the low mean P.I.L. scores of the Indian samples are surprising and should be a cause of serious concern.

But in the opinion of the present investigator the low Indian P.I.L. score may be of serious concern but it is not surprising. In the absence of norms for Western and Indian groups, truthful comparison may not be advisable. One strong criticism against psychometric tools is the low correlation values between tools. It is because of ambiguity in the statements (test items) and difficulty in understanding some statements (Kelly 1974). The P.I.L. is no exception. When such a tool is administered to a non-English population, these reasons may explain that difference of about 15 points in the mean P.I.L. scores between the Indian groups and Western groups. Whether it is 118 or 99 it does not indicate high in meaning in life in a scale range of 20-140. These groups may be considered as either moderate or low though they are not as low as to be considered psychic cases. This rather low meaning in life experienced by the Indian youth, represented in this case by the prospective teachers can also be explained as follows.

Weisskoef and Joelson while explaining Frankl's approach to existential therapy described that the unhappiness in 20th century is a syndrome of existential vacuum characterized by boredom, emptiness, lack of direction, and ignorance regarding what to do with one's life. They further say that paucity of close relationships in the modern society, absence of shared vision of a better life in a future, focus of material aspects of life and the neglect of the spiritual aspects are some of the factors associated with loss of meaning in life in the American youth.

Today the Indian society has reached this stage and the Indian youth are facing the similar societal condition. Among this youth those who come to the preparatory course of teacher education are usually considered as the ones who are catching the last straw of opportunity. Hence their low meaning in life expressed in P.I.L. scores is not surprising. It will be enlightening if we know whether the Indian youth preparing for other professions and jobs are also on the same level.

It is a matter of concern that the prospective teachers are low in meaning in life as revealed in this investigation and their mentors that is the teacher educators are also on the same level as found in the earlier studies of Misra and Mohanty. If both the teacher and the teacher educator are on the verge of pathological condition, who will attend to the mental health of the coming generation of teachers?

In conclusion it can be said that the prospective teachers, who are a segment of the modern Indian young society, are experiencing loss of meaning in life which is revealed in the low P.I.L. mean score. It is also observed in this investigation that prospective men and women teachers are almost on the same level of loss of meaning in life. This is revealed from their P.I.L. mean scores 99.53 for men and 98.98 for women. Based on the principle of mean ± 1 S.D., the total sample is categorized into three levels, namely, low in meaning in life, moderate in meaning in life and high in meaning in life. The limits for this classification are given below.

Low in meaning in life = 83 and below

High in meaning in life = 116 and above

Moderate in meaning in life = 84 to 115.

The distribution of the sample in these three categories is given in Table—4.2.

Table—4.2 Distribution of the sample—Three categories—P.I.L.

Category	*Limit*	*N*
Low	83 and below	60
High	116 and above	40
Moderate	84-115	230
Total		**330**

The data in the above table is diagrammatically represented in Fig. No. 4.1.

Fig. 4.1

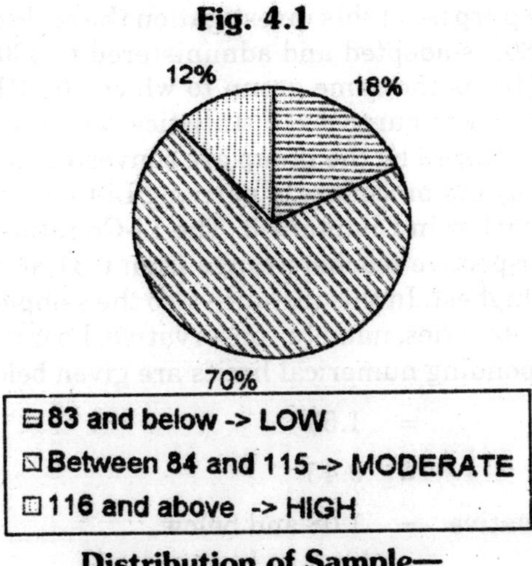

**Distribution of Sample—
Categories—Purpose in Life**

This categorization is done assuming that the P.I.L. scores are normal to the prospective teachers in Andhra Pradesh in India. No other basis of classification is possible in the absence of norms for either Indian groups or foreign groups. Within the limits of the sample scores, it can be said that above 70 per cent of prospective teachers are moderate in meaning in life, 19 per cent are low in meaning in life while only 11 per cent are highly in meaning in life.

Nature of the Sample in Terms of Educational Philosophic Beliefs

In this context of educational philosophic beliefs, it is supposed to identify the sample as liberals and conservatives. It should be recalled that classification such as liberal-conservative and democratic autocratic are not absolute. It is assumed that nobody is either purely conservative or purely liberal. One is identified as liberal if his beliefs are predominantly liberal and one is considered as conservative, if his beliefs are predominantly conservative. In other words an individual will be located somewhere on the liberal-conservative continuum when measured on Educational Liberalism-Conservatism Scale. (E.L.C.S.).

For the purpose of this investigation the scale developed by Sastry (1980) is adopted and administered to 330 prospective teachers. This is the same group to which the P.I.L. was also administered. For purposes of statistical analysis of the data, the scores obtained by the group are converted to Li-Co ratios. The meaning and procedure of deriving Li-Co ratios have been explained earlier in Chapter—3. The Li-Co ratios obtained by the 330 prospective teachers range from 0.31 at the lowest to 3.51 at the highest. In this instance also the sample is classified into three categories, namely, conservative, liberal and eclectic. The corresponding numerical limits are given below:

Mean = 1.53

σ = 0.45

Conservative = 1.08 and below

Liberal = 1.98 and above

Eclectic = 1.09 to 1.97

The category-wise distribution of the sample is presented in Table—4.3.

Table—4.3 Distribution of the sample—Three categories—beliefs

Category	*Numerical limits*	*N*
Conservative	1.08 and below	51
Liberal	1.98 and above	49
Eclectic	1.09 to 1.97	230
Total		**330**

The eclectic group represent the people who cannot be classified either as conservatives or liberals when conservatism and liberalism are defined in terms of the numerical limits given above. From the data in the above table, it can be seen that about 70 per cent of the sample population are eclectic. Conservatives and liberals and present in the sample up to 15 per cent each. Though young people might have developed conservative or liberal outlook towards life in general, the people who are still undergoing teacher training may not be able to follow definite attitudes towards teaching and teaching practices. This might be the cause for the presence of vast majority of prospective teachers in the eclectic category.

The data presented so far to describe the nature of the sample group of this investigation in terms of purpose in life and educational philosophic beliefs has been subjected to further statistical treatment and analysis in order to describe interrelationships and to verify the hypotheses.

The results are reported hypothesiswise in the following pages.

H_1: *Meaning in life held by prospective teachers has no relationship with the philosophical beliefs.*

To test this hypothesis the coefficient of correlation has been computed between scores obtained by the sample on P.I.L. and E.L.C.S. using product moment correlation technique. The obtained r is 0.07. Test of significance has been calculated. It is found that the obtained "r" value 0.07 is not significant at 0.05 level.

To verify this result, further statistical treatment is given to the data. It is proposed to subject the data to Chi Square test of independence. For this purpose, null hypothesis was constructed. To test this hypothesis, the table of joint frequencies of sample population distributed on the P.I.L. and Li-Co ratios is prepared and the Chi Square of independence has been conducted on the data. The results are shown in Table—4.4.

Table—4.4 P.I.L. and Li-co Ratio Chi square test (Table of joint frequencies)

P.I.L.	*Conservative 1.08 and less*	*Eclectic between 1.09 to 1.97*	*Liberal 1.98 & above*	*Total*
Low 83 or less	9 (9.2)	45 (41.40)	6 (8.82)	60
Moderate between 84 to 115	37 (35.55)	161 (161)	32 (34.3)	230
High 116	5 (6.10)	24 (27.60)	11 (5.88)	40
Total	**51**	**230**	**49**	**330**

The obtained Chi square value for the data in Table—4.4 is 6.59. The table value for 4 d.f. is 9.488 at 0.05 level. So the obtained 'F' value is not significant.

Hence the null hypothesis is retained. It can be said that the evidence produced with the sample and under the conditions of this investigation is not sufficient to establish relationship between philosophic beliefs of prospective teachers and their levels of P.I.L.

> H_2: *The correlation values of M.I.L. and educational philosophic beliefs for men significantly differ from those for women.*

Some earlier investigations with P.I.L. suggested that men find meaning in societal situation, i.e. comfort, fun, money, etc. while women usually find meaning in humanistic situation, i.e., affection, love, patience etc. This has led the investigator to believe that the relationship between P.I.L. and educational philosophic beliefs found in men prospective teachers might be significantly different from the relationship as exists in women prospective teachers, even though it is already reported that there is no relationship between P.I.L. and educational philosophic beliefs when the total sample population is considered. To verify this theory related to hypothesis II the following procedure is adopted. P.I.L. and Li Co ratios of men and women sample have been listed separately. Correlation coefficient between P.I.L. and Li-Co ratios of men is computed, (r_1). Similarly r_2 for women is also computed. The significance of difference between r_1 and r_2 has been calculated. The results are given in Table—4.5.

Table—4.5 Li-co ratios and P.I.L. scores—Correlations in men and women

Variables	*Coefficient of correlation*	*N*	*Z*	*D*	*o z_1-z_2*	*C.R.*
Men	0.26	168	0.27	0.19	0.11	1.73*
Women	0.08	162	0.08			

* Not significant at 0.05 level.

The obtained C.R. value, 1.73 is not significant at 0.05 level. Hence it is concluded that there is no significant difference in the relationship between P.I.L. and educational philosophic beliefs as they are found in men and women prospective teachers.

H_3: There is a positive correlation between Li Co-ratios and their P.I.L. scores of liberals on E.L.C.S.

In the process of testing the first hypothesis it is found that around two-thirds of the sample population are in the eclectic group of philosophical beliefs and moderate in purpose of life. The remaining less than one-third of the sample is distributed in the extremes. Hence the investigator is led to think that though the calculations on the whole group has not established conclusive relationship between philosophical beliefs and purpose in life, statistical association may be found when extreme groups are treated separately. Hence the hypothesis and the subsequent one are formulated.

There are 49 prospective teachers in the liberal group in a sample of 330. Their scores on P.I.L. and E.L.C.S. have been taken separately and coefficient of correlation was computed. The obtained r = 0.06 is not significant at 0.05 level.

Hence it is concluded that there is no relation between liberal philosophic beliefs and level of purpose in life. The research hypothesis is not supported by the evidence.

H_4: Prospective teachers who are conservative on the Li Co= ratios scale score low on the P.I.L. scale.

There are 51 prospective teachers falling in the conservative side of the E.L.C.S. coefficient of correlation for their Li Co ratios and P.I.L. scores was computed. The obtained r is –0.14. Negative correlation indicates that those who are high on one measure will be low on the other measure and vice-versa. Though the obtained value, –0.14, is not statistically significant, the negative value points towards the relationship between conservative and level of P.I.L. which is assumed in the hypothesis.

However, the results reported above is contrary to the contentions of Misra and Mohanty. They reason that Indians are generally conservatives. Conservatives up-hold traditional values strongly! Those who hold certain values strongly do not easily fall into the experience of meaninglessness (low P.I.L. scores). This investigation shows that the presence of conservatives at least as far as Andhra Pradesh sample is concerned is not large. Against their contention, it is also found in this investigation that there is negative relation between purpose in life and conservatism instead of positive relationship.

However, this comparison should not be stretched further leading to any final conclusion.

The Andhra Pradesh sample of this investigation is culturally different from the Calcutta and Orissa sample groups of Misra and Mohanty. Their age and employment status differences are also to be noted. Even Western studies dealing with P.I.L. and burnout (M.B.I. scale) have indicated that different studies with different demographic characteristics like geographical location, age, and nature of work have varied influences on purpose in life and burnout experiences and a lot of in-depth research is still needed to establish norms for P.I.L. for different demographic groups.

The findings of this investigation also points out this need.

H_5: Sex makes differences in the level of experience of purpose in life.

To test this hypothesis, it is proposed to compare the mean scores obtained by the men and women prospective teachers on P.I.L. and to compute C.R. to find out the significance of difference. The H_6 framed for this hypothesis is given below:

H_6: The mean P.I.L. scores obtained by men and women do not differ.

The results of statistical treatment are reported in Table—4.6.

Table—4.6 Mean comparison of sex X P.I.L.

Variable	*N*	*Mean*	*S.D.*	*D*	σ_D	*C.R.*
Men	168	99.53	15.52	0.55	1.77	0.31
Women	162	98.98	16.69			

The obtained C.R. value, 0.31, is not statistically significant at 0.05 level. Hence the null hypothesis has to be retained. It is to be said that there is no conclusive evidence to support the research hypothesis. It can be observed that among prospective teachers of Andhra Pradesh there is no difference between men and women in their level of experience of purpose in life.

H_6: Sex makes difference in the expressed educational philosophic beliefs.

Until two decades ago, within the Indian context, it is said by people, both scholars and common men alike, that women were more conservative than men in their attitude to life. But during the past five to six years a number of articles appeared in newspapers and journals based on media opinion poll type research which described young girls expressing more liberal opinions about sex, marital life, lift style, work place ethics, going abroad, etc.. Several articles by Sevanti Ninan appearing in *The Hindu* during 1995-96 serve as example to these observations. Review of such articles motivated this investigator to find out if among the present-day teacher trainees also women and men differ in their educational philosophic beliefs. Hence the above hypothesis has been formulated.

To test this hypothesis, it is proposed to compare the mean scores obtained by the men and women prospective teachers on philosophical beliefs as measured on E.L.C.S. and to compute C.R. to find out the significance of difference. The H_0 framed for this hypothesis is given below.

H_0: The mean Li Co ratio scores obtained by men and women do not differ significantly.

The results of statistical treatment are reported in Table—4.7.

Table—4.7 Mean comparison of Sex X E.L.C.S.

Variable	*N*	*Mean*	*S.D.*	*D*	σ_D	*C.R.*
Men	168	1.51	0.46			
Women	162	1.52	0.42	0.01	0.049	0.20

The obtained C.R. value 0.20 is not statistically significant at 0.05 level. Hence the null hypothesis has to be retained. It must be said that there is no conclusive evidence to support the research hypothesis. It may be inferred that among the prospective teachers of Andhra Pradesh there is no difference between men and women in their level of educational philosophic beliefs.

The interpretation of the finding requires care and logic. The statistics here revealed only that there is no significant difference in the educational philosophic beliefs of women and men teacher trainees. When measured on E.L.C.S. from this it cannot be concluded that this is contrary to the findings of Sevanty Ninan and others as reported in newspaper reports that women are emerging on liberals and coming out of their traditional conservative shell. In this context it should be recalled that while describing the nature of the sample in this investigation in terms of categories of P.I.L. and E.L.C.S., over 70 per cent the sample teacher trainees, both men and women are in the eclectic category. Precisely, out of the total sample of 330 prospective teachers, 168 are men and 162 are women. Out of the 330 sample, 230 are in the eclectic category. The eclectic category people are in the middle of the E.L.C. scale with conservatives on the lower extreme and liberals are on the higher extreme. For ready reference the data is graphically shown in Fig. No. 4.2.

Fig. 4.2

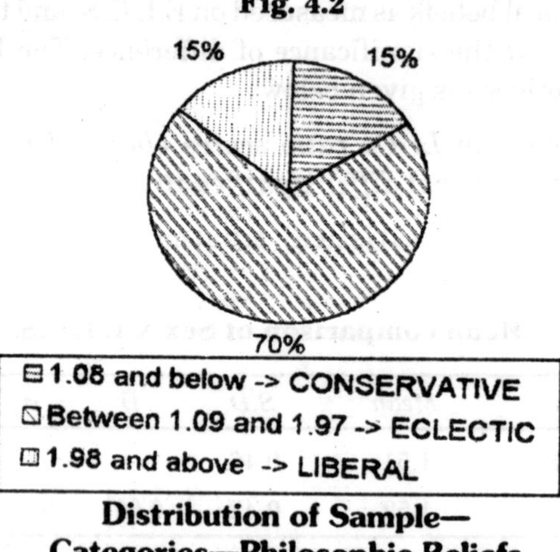

Distribution of Sample—Categories—Philosophic Beliefs

Reading the statistical data in this hypothesis and the sample population characteristic together, it is logically derived that men and women perspective teachers do not differ significantly in their philosophic beliefs and a large majority of both are in the eclectic category of E.L.C.S. From this it logically follows that women teacher trainees in considerable percentage have emerged out of the conservative shell. This indicates the theory behind this hypothesis, though further research is needed to empirically confirm this logical derivative but which is beyond the scope of this investigation.

H_7: *The mean scores on P.I.L. scale obtained by prospective teachers with mathematics, biological sciences and social sciences background differ.*

The people who joined teacher training fall into three categories depending on the main subject of study in their entry qualification, i.e. first degree course, namely, mathematics, biological sciences and social sciences. Since their respective foundation studies in intermediate (higher secondary) itself, youngsters both boys and girls hold varying levels of the future prospects relative to the major subject in which they are able to secure seats. Thus, for example, depending on the present-day economic statuses for different jobs and professions in our society, people who could secure seats in biological sciences with an ambition to become medicos, generally consider themselves fortunate and experience high meaning in life. On the other hand, the residuals, who remain in humanities, find loss of meaning in life. Hence it is hypothesised that differences in entry qualifications of teacher trainees will be associated with difference in their P.I.L. scores. To verify this, the following H_0 was constructed as stated below.

H_0: *The mean scores on P.I.L. scale obtained by prospective teachers with mathematics, biological sciences and social sciences background do not differ significantly.*

To test this hypothesis, ANOVA was computed. Results are tabulated in Table—4.8.

Table—4.8 P.I.L. variables X subject variables—ANOVA

Source of variation	*d.f.*	*Sum of squares*	*Variance*	*F-ratio*
Among the means of conditions	2	159.95	79.98	0.31
Within conditions	327	84736.11	259.13	

The table value for d.f. 2 and 327, at 0.05 level of significance, is 19.50. The obtained 'F' value is 0.31, which is less than the table value. Hence it is not significant at 0.05 level. As a result the null hypothesis is retained. In other words, due to the subject of study (mathematics or biological sciences or social studies) in their entry qualification, the mean P.I.L. scores of the prospective teachers do not differ significantly.

> H_8: *Mathematics, biological sciences and social sciences teacher trainees differ in their philosophic beliefs.*

The trainees fall into three categories according to their optional methodology which again are based on the main subject of study in their first degree, namely, mathematics, biological sciences and social sciences. Generally it is believed that students with three or more years of specialization in those subjects associated with instruction methodology in B.Ed. course may develop different sets of notions regarding values of life, disciplines etc. From this stand-point, the argument is extended that trainees coming out of these three streams differ in their educational beliefs.

> H_0: *Mathematics, biological sciences and social sciences teacher trainees do not differ in their philosophic beliefs.*

Statistical technique used: ANOVA

Table—4.9 Methodology subjects—Philosophic beliefs—ANOVA

Source of variation	*d.f.*	*Sum of squares*	*Variance*	*F-ratio*
Among the means of conditions	2	0.96	0.48	2.4
Within conditions	327	65.16	0.20	

The table value for d.f. 2 and 327, at 0.05 level of significance is 19.50. The obtained 'F' value is 2.4 which is less than the table value. Hence it is not significant at 0.05 level. As a result the null hypothesis is retained. In other words due to the subject of study and optimal methodology (mathematics or biological sciences or social sciences) the mean Li Co ratio scores of the prospective teachers do not differ significantly.

The results of this investigation reported above have contradicted the rationale behind this hypothesis. It needs some explanation. The curricula in the undergraduate and post-graduate courses in our country still follow the British educational model of the Victorian age. Besides the subject of specialization, a lot of common core curriculum is there in the name of languages and Indian culture, science and civilization etc. All these combine to produce confusible mind. This might be the reason the majority of the sample are in the eclectic category of the E.L.C.S. The influence of specialised subject might not be strong enough to produce differences in the philosophic outlook of the sample. Of course conditions outside the educational system also contribute to this phenomena.

SUMMARY, CONCLUSIONS AND SUGGESTIONS

The present investigation proposed to study the relationship between purpose in life and educational philosophic beliefs of prospective teachers. Frankl developed the concept of meaning in life. Based on this Crumbaugh and Maholick developed the purpose in life scale to measure the level of meaning in life experienced by individuals. Educational philosophic beliefs are the beliefs of people in the teaching profession towards education and educational practices.

There are several philosophies of education. The investigator, for convenience of measurement, has taken into consideration the more comprehensive dichotomy of conservative-liberal conservative scale (E.L.C.S.) to measure the educational philosophic beliefs of persons in the teaching profession. These two tools are selected by the investigator to get data necessary for realising the objectives of this study.

Objectives of the Study

This investigation was conducted with the following objectives.

1. To find out if the level of meaning in life held by the prospective teachers have any relation to the philosophic beliefs.

2. To find out if sex and purpose in life held by the teacher trainees are related.
3. To find out if the subjects of study at graduation have any relation to the P.I.L. held by the prospective teachers.
4. To find out if sex and philosophic beliefs of prospective teachers are related.
5. To find out if the subjects of study in the basic *D* degree of the prospective teachers and their philosophic beliefs are related.

Hypotheses of the Study

1. Experienced level of meaning in life of prospective teachers has relationship with the philosophic beliefs.
2. Prospective teachers who are liberal on the Li-Co ratio score high on the P.I.L. scale.
3. Prospective teachers who are conservative on the Li-Co ratio scores stand low on the P.I.L. scale.
4. The mean P.I.L. scores obtained by men and women differ.
5. The mean scores on P.I.L. scale obtained by the three groups of trainees in terms of entry classification, viz. mathematics, biological sciences and social sciences differ.
6. Men and women prospective teachers differ in their philosophic beliefs in terms Li-Co Ratios.
7. Mathematics, biological sciences and social sciences teacher trainees differ in their philosophic beliefs expressed in terms Li-Co Ratios.

Administration of the Tool

The two tools were administered to the teacher trainees of four college of education in Krishna Dt. of Andhra Pradesh. The sample of the study consisted of three hundred and thirty teacher trainees from these colleges of education.

The P.I.L. is a non-timed self administering scale and the total score is the sum of the numerical values circled for the 20 items, therefore the score can theoretically range from 20 to 140.

In the case of E.L.C.S. liberalism conservatism ratio (Li-Co ratio) was computed for each individual teacher.

$$\text{Li-Co Ratio} = \frac{\text{Proportion of agreed items under liberal philosophy of education}}{\text{Proportion of agreed items under conservative philosophy of education.}}$$

Statistical Technique Adopted

Coefficient of correlation between P.I.L. and Li-Co ratio scores was calculated. Means and standard deviations were computed for Li-Co and P.I.L. scores separately and critical ratio was computed to test the significant difference between men and women prospective teachers. ANOVA was adopted to test the significant difference among the three groups (mathematics, biological sciences and social studies) for P.I.L. scores and Li-Co ratio separately. The major findings from the analysis of this data are given hereunder.

Findings

1. The prospective teachers who are a segment of the modern Indian young society are experiencing rather loss of meaning in life. This is evident from mean score of 99.41 for the total sample on the P.I.L. scale.

2. It is found that there is no statistically significant difference between the P.I.C. — E.L.C.S., 'r' for men and 'r' for women.

3. Prospective men and women teachers are almost on the same level of loss of meaning in life.

4. Seventy per cent of the prospective teachers are moderate on meaning in life, 19 per cent are low in meaning in life, while only 11 per cent are high in meaning in life.

5. About 70 per cent of the sample population are eclectic. Conservatives and liberals are present in the sample upto 15 per cent each (educational philosophic beliefs).
6. Meaning in life held by prospective teachers has no relationship to their educational philosophic beliefs.
7. There is no relation between conservative philosophic beliefs and level of purpose in life.
8. There is no relation between liberal philosophic beliefs and level of purpose in life.

Suggestions

I. Psychometricians like Aikem and Kelly maintained that when the null hypothesis is rejected the research hypothesis automatically accepted, but the converse is not true. The acceptance of null hypothesis need not always lead to the rejection of the research hypothesis automatically. The null hypothesis is accepted under the specific conditions with which it is constructed. But the research hypothesis might be under the impact of several other conditions. (spurious conditions). Until all those conditions or atleast the important conditions are tested the existence of differences proposed in the research hypothesis can't be rejected hence it is suggested that an in-depth study of the purpose in life and educational philosophic beliefs taking into consideration, the factors contributed to them one necessary before acceptance or rejection of the relationship between purpose in life and educational philosophic beliefs.

II. This study replicated with the sample of in-service teachers will also produce interesting results.

III. Even in the West, there is a criticism of the purpose in life scale of Crumbaugh. It is said that the language of some of the items is difficult and ambiguous. With Indian respondents the difficulty should be greater. When such a drawback exists the respondents simply pick-out one of the alternative responses by chance but not by choice. In such cases the psychometric tool can not project the personality trait or a human characteristic of respondents. This explains the consistently low mean P.I.L. score of Indian samples and strongly suggests the need for translated or improved version of the P.I.L. scale suitable for Indian conditions.

BIBLIOGRAPHY

Black, W.A.M. and Gregson, R.A.M. (1973), Time Perspective, Purpose in Life, Extraversion and Neuroticism in Newzealand Prisoners. *British Journal of Social and Clinical Psychology*, 12.

Brameld, T (1955), Philosophies of Education in Cultural Perspective," New York: The Dryden Press.

Brameld, T (1971), Patterns of Educational Philosophy: Divergence and Convergence—*Anthrological Perspective*, New York: Holt, Rinehort and Winston.

Butler, J.D. (1951), "Four Philosophies and their Practices in Education and Religion" New York: Harper Bros.

Butler, A. and Carr, L. (1968), Purpose in Life through Social Action, *Journal of Social Psychology*, 74.

Crandal, J and Rasmussen, R. (1975), Purpose in Life as Related to Specific Values, *Journal of Clinical Psychology*, 31. 15.

Crumbaugh, J. (1968), Cross Validation of Purpose in Life Test Based on Frankl's Concept. *Journal of Individual Psychology*, 24.

Crumbaugh, J. and Maholick, L. (1964), An Experimental Study in Existentialism: The Psychometric Approach to Frankl's Concept of Noogenic Neurosis, *Journal of Clinical Psychology*, 20.

Crumbaugh, J. and Maholick, L. (1969), Manual of Instruction for the Purpose in Life Test, *Munster, Psychometric Affiliates*.

Crumbaugh, J., Raphael, M. and Sharder, R. (1970), Frankl's will to Meaning in Religious Order, *Journal of Clinical Psychology*, 26.23.

Doerris, L. (1970), Purpose in Life and Social Participation, *Journal of Individual Psychology*, Vol. 26.35.

Dupuis (1972), *Philosophy of Education in Historical Perspective,* New Delhi: Thomson Press (India) Ltd.

Edith Weisskopef Joelson (1978), *Six Representative Approaches to Existential Therapy—(A) Viktor Frankl*, in Valle R.S. and Markinny, "Existential Phenomenological Alternatives for Psychology," New York: Ford University Press.

Familetti, M. (1975), A Comparison of the Meaning and Purpose in Life of Delinquent High School Boys, *Dissertation Abstracts International*, Vol. 36.

Gaind and Sharma (1973), *Educational Theories and Modern Trends,* Agra: Ramprasad Sons.

Gon, M. and Mehta, P. (1982), *A Comparative Study of Purpose in Life among Physically Disabled and Non-Disabled Men and Women*. Proceedings of 69th Session of the Indian Science Congress Association, University of Mysore.

Good, C.V. (Ed.) (1959), *Dictionary of Education*, New York: Mc Graw Hill Book Co.

Hansen, K.H. (1960), *Philosophy for American Education,* Englewood Cliffs: Prentice Hall.

Hunt, M.P. (1975), *Foundations of Education—Social and Cultural Perspectives,* New York: Holt, Rinehort and Winston.

Jacobson, R. and Ritter. D. (1977), Purpose in Life and Personal Values among Adult Alcoholics. *Journal of Clinical Psychology*, 3366.

Jagannadha Rao, K. (1971), *A Critical Study of the Educational Philosophy of Teachers Working in Secondary Schools,* Unpublished M.Ed. Dissertation, Andhra University.

Jain, B.K., *The Philosophy of Education as Held by Some of the Teacher Educators in U.P. and Delhi*. Summaries of Report, Central Institute of Education, Publication No. 57.

Kerlinger, F.N (1967), *Social Attitudes and their Critical Referents:* A Structural Theory, Psychological Review, 74.

Kerliner, F.N. and Kaya, E. (1959), The Construction and Factor Analytic Validation of Scales to Measure Attitudes toward Education, *Educational and Psychological Measurement*, 19.

Kneller, G.F. (1967), *Introduction to the Philosophy of Education*, New York: John Wiley Sons.

Kotchen, T.A. (1960), Existential Mental Health, An Empirical Approach, *Journal of Individual Psychology*, 16 (2).

Krech and Crutchfield (1948), *Theory and Problem of Social Psychology,* Bombay: Tata McGraw Hill Publishing Co.

Miller, R.S. (1963), Educators' Attitudes toward Educational Practices, *The Journal of Educational Research,* Vol. 56, No. 8.

Mohanty, R.K. (1990), *A Study of Meaning in Life, Burnoutness and Work Orientation of Teacher Educators of Orissa,* Unpublished Ph.D. Thesis, Baroda: C.A.S.E., M.S. University.

Oliver, W.A. (1970), Teacher's Educational Beliefs Versus their Classroom Practices, In Morse and Wingo (Eds.) *"Reading in Educational Psychology*, Bombay: D.B. Tara- Porevala Sons and Co.

Oliver, and Butcher (1962), Teacher's Attitudes to Education: The Structure of Educational Attitude, *British Journal of Social and Clinical Psychology,* 1.

Padleford, B. (1972), Relationship between Drug Involvement and Purpose in Life, *Journal of Clinical Psychology*, Vol. 30.

Pramod Kumar (1978), A Comparative Study of Educational Attitudes, *Journal of Educational Research and Extension*. Vol. 15, No. 1.

Rude, J.S., (1981), Meaning in Life As a Function of School and Non-School Variables in Adolescent Males, *Dissertation Abstracts International*, Vol. 41.

Sastry, D.S.N. (1980), *A Study of the Classroom Behaviour of Teachers in relation to their Philosophic Beliefs in Education,* Unpublished Ph.D. Thesis, Andhra University.

Seshadri, C. (1977), *Philosophy of Education—A Trend Report,* in Fifth Survey of Educational Research, New Delhi, N.C.E.R.T.

Shean, B. and Fechtmann, F. (1971), Purpose in Life Scores of Student Marijuna Users. *Journal of Clinical Psychology,* Vol. 27.

Smith B.O. (1960), Philosophy of Education in *Encyclopaedia of Educational Research* edited by Harris, C.M., New York: The Macmillan Company.

Steliner and Fishbein, *Current Studies in Social Psychology,* New York: Holt, Rinehort and Winston.

Sultana, A. (1983), *A Study of Some Factors in Adjustment Pattern of Adolescent Boys and Girls in Bangladesh,* Unpublished Doctoral Thesis. Baroda: C.A.S.E., M.S. University.

Victor, J.B. (1976), Relation between Teacher Belief and Teacher Personality in Four Samples of Teacher Trainees, *The Journal of Experimental Education*, Vol. 45, No. 1.

Wingo, G.M. (1975), *Philosophies of Education: An Introduction,* New Delhi: Sterling Publishers.

Yarnell, T. (1971), Purpose in Life Test—Further Correlates, *Journal of Individual Psychology*, Vol. 27.

ADDITIONAL READING

Bhaskara Rao, Digumarti (1994). *Scientific Aptitude*, New Delhi: Ashish Publishing House. pp. 100. ISBN 81-7024-658-X.

Bhaskara Rao, Digumarti (1995). *Animal Kingdom*. New Delhi: Discovery Publishing House. pp. 135. ISBN 81-7141-274-2.

Bhaskara Rao, Digumarti (1995). *Batracology*. New Delhi: Discovery Publishing House. pp. 174. ISBN 81-7141-279-3.

Bhaskara Rao, Digumarti (1996). *Scientific Attitude vis-à-vis Scientific Aptitude*. New Delhi: Discovery Publishing House. pp. 143. ISBN 81-7141-308-0.

Bhaskara Rao, Digumarti, Editor (1996). *Encyclopaedia of Education for All,* 5 Volumes. New Delhi: APH Publishing Corporation. pp. 1460. ISBN 81-7024-759-4 (set).

Vol. I *Education for All: The World Conference*. pp. 440. ISBN 81-7024-760-8.

Vol. II *Education for All: The EPA-9 Summit*. pp. 340. ISBN 81-7024-761-6.

Vol. III *Education for All: Quality Education for All*. pp. 250. ISBN 81-7024-762-6.

Vol. IV *Education for All: Planning and Monitoring*. pp. 170. ISBN 81-7024-763-4.

Vol. V *Education for All: The Indian Scenario*. pp. 260. ISBN 81-7024-764-0.

Bhaskara Rao, Digumarti, Editor (1996). *Global Perceptions on Peace Education,* 3 Volumes. New Delhi: Discovery Publishing House. pp. 980. ISBN 81-7141-319-6.

Bhaskara Rao, Digumarti, Editor (1996). *National Policy on Education*. 2 Volumes. New Delhi: Anmol Publications Pvt. Ltd. pp. 710. ISBN 81-7488-323-1.

Bhaskara Rao, Digumarti, Editor (1997). *Care the Child*, 2 Volumes. New Delhi: Discovery Publishing House. pp. 616. ISBN 81-7141-394-3.

Bhaskara Rao, Digumarti, Editor (1997). *Education for the 21st Century*. New Delhi: Discovery Publishing House. pp. 288. ISBN 81-7141-389-7.

Bhaskara Rao, Digumarti, Editor (1997). *Reflections on Scientific Attitude*. New Delhi: Discovery Publishing House, pp. 980. ISBN 81-7141-319-6.

Bhaskara Rao, Digumarti (1997). *Scientific Attitude*. New Delhi: Discovery Publishing House. pp. 120. ISBN 81-7141-381-1.

Bhaskara Rao, Digumarti, Editor (1997). *Success Story of a Primary Education Project*. New Delhi: APH Publishing Corporation. pp. 260. ISBN 81-7024-850-7.

Bhaskara Rao, Digumarti, Editor (1997). *World Food Summit*. New Delhi: Discovery Publishing House. pp. 153. ISBN 81-7141-386-2.

Bhaskara Rao, Digumarti, Editor (1998). *Adolescence Education*. New Delhi: Discovery Publishing House. pp. 238. ISBN 81-7141-432-X.

Bhaskara Rao, Digumarti, Editor (1998). *Community and School Nutrition Education*. New Delhi: Discovery Publishing House. pp. 425. ISBN 81-7141-435-4.

Bhaskara Rao, Digumarti, Editor (1998). *District Primary Education Programme*. New Delhi: Discovery Publishing House. pp. 506. ISBN 81-7141-396-X.

Bhaskara Rao, Digumarti, Editor (1998). *Earth Summit*, 2 Volumes. New Delhi: Discovery Publishing House. pp. 930. ISBN 81-7141-435-4.

Bhaskara Rao, Digumarti, Editor (1998). *National Policy on Education: Towards an Enlightened and Humane Society*, New Delhi: Discovery Publishing House. pp. 542. ISBN 81-7141-426-5.

Bhaskara Rao, Digumarti, Editor (1998). *Reforming School Education*. New Delhi: Discovery Publishing House. pp. 575. ISBN 81-7141-403-6.

Bhaskara Rao, Digumarti, Editor (1998). *Teacher Education in India*. New Delhi: Discovery Publishing House. pp. 424. ISBN 81-7141-406-0.

Bhaskara Rao, Digumarti, Editor (1998). *World Summit for Social Development*. New Delhi: Discovery Publishing House. pp. 278. ISBN 81-7141-420-6.

Bhaskara Rao, Digumarti, Editor (2000). *Education for All: Achieving the Goal*, 3 Volumes, New Delhi: APH Publishing Corporation. pp. 830. ISBN 81-7648-152-1.

Vol. I *The Global Consensus*. pp. 285. ISBN 81-7648-155-6.

Vol. II *Mid-Decade Review Reports of Regional Seminars*. pp. 198. ISBN 81-7648-154-8.

Vol. III *Issues and Trends*. pp. 346. ISBN 81-7648-155-6.

Bhaskara Rao, Digumarti, Editor (2000), *International Encyclopaedia of AIDS*, 11 Volumes in 13 Parts. New Delhi: Discovery Publishing House. pp. 676. ISBN 81-7141-6 (Set).

Vol. 1 *Introduction to HIV/AIDS*. pp. 246. ISBN 81-7141-523-7.

Vol. 2 *HIV/AIDS—Issues and Challenges*, 2 Parts. pp. 805. ISBN 81-7141-524-5.

Vol. 3 *HIV/AIDS—Socio Economic Realities*. pp. 436. ISBN 81-7141-524-3.

Vol. 4 *HIV/AIDS—Law Ethics and Human Rights*, 2 Parts. pp. 589. ISBN 81-7141-526-1.

Vol. 5 *AIDS and NGOs*. pp. 215. ISBN 81-7141-527-X.

Vol. 6 *AIDS and Home Care*. pp. 183. ISBN 81-7141-528-8.

Vol. 7 *STD Case Management*. pp. 223. ISBN 81-7141-529-6.

Vol. 8 *HIV/AIDS Prevention and Care—Teaching Modules for Nurses and Midwives*. pp. 183. ISBN 81-7141-530-X.

Vol. 9 *HIV Prevention Education for Education for Educational Institutions*. pp. 75. ISBN 81-7141-531-8.

Vol. 10 *Instructional Modules for AIDS Education*. pp. 111. ISBN 81-7141-532-6.

Vol. 11 *School Health Education to Prevent AIDS and STD—A Package for Curriculum Planners*. pp. 298. ISBN 81-7141-5338-4.

Bhaskara Rao, Digumarti, Editor (2000). *International Encyclopaedia of Science and Technology Education*, 11 Volumes. New Delhi: Discovery Publishing House. pp. 4892. ISBN 81-7141-548-2 (Set).

Vol. 1 *Science and Technology Education*. pp. 557. ISBN 81-7141-568-7.

Vol. 2 *Science Education in Developing Countries*. pp. 334. ISBN 81-7141-570-9.

Vol. 3 *Organisational Structure of Science*. pp. 334. ISBN 81-7141-570-9.

Vol. 4 *Science Education in Asia and the Pacific*. pp. 249. ISBN 81-7141-571-7.

Vol. 5 *Science and Technology Education for All*. pp. 464. ISBN 81-7141-572-5.

Vol. 6 *Values, Ethics, Talent and Girls in Science and Technology Education*. pp. 463. ISBN 81-7141-573-3.

Vol. 7 *Popularization of Science and Technology Education*. pp. 334. ISBN 81-7141-574-1.

Vol. 8 *Science, Power and Society*. pp. 357. ISBN 81-7141-575-X.

Vol. 9 *Information Technology*. pp. 442. Rs. 775. ISBN 81-7141-576-8.

Vol. 10 *Teacher Training in Science and Technology Education*. pp. 536. ISBN 81-7141-577-6.

Vol. 11 *Teacher Training in Science and Technology: A Curriculum Framework*. pp. 642. ISBN 81-7141-578-4.

Bhaskara Rao, Digumarti, Editor (2001). *Distance Education in Different Countries*. New Delhi: APH Publishing Corporation. pp. 574. ISBN 81-7648-229-3.

Bhaskara Rao, Digumarti, Editor (2001). *Decentralised Management of Education (Management of Education in Panchayati Raj and Municipal Bodies)*. New Delhi: Discovery Publishing House. pp. 116. ISBN 81-7141-617-9.

Bhaskara Rao, Digumarti, Editor (2001). *Electrochemistry for Environmental Protection*. New Delhi: Discovery Publishing House. pp. 208. ISBN 81-7141-619-5.

Bhaskara Rao, Digumarti, Editor (2001). *Global Educational Studies*. New Delhi: Discovery Publishing House. pp. 145. ISBN 81-7141-616-0.

Bhaskara Rao, Digumarti, Editor (2001). *Global Synthesis of Educational Assessment*. New Delhi: Discovery Publishing House. pp. 152. ISBN 81-7141-613-6.

Bhaskara Rao, Digumarti, Editor (2000). *International Encyclopaedia of Human Rights*. 7 Volumes in 13 Parts. New Delhi: Discovery Publishing House. pp. 6500 (Royal Size). ISBN 81-7141-567-9 (Set).

Vol. 1 *International Instruments of Human Rights*, 2 Parts. ISBN 81-7141-595-4.

Vol. 2 *Regional Instruments of Human Rights*. ISBN 81-7141-604-7.

Vol. 3 *Human Rights and the United Nations*, 2 Parts. ISBN 81-7141-605-5.

Vol. 4 *Fact Files of Human Rights*, 3 Parts. ISBN 81-7141-605-3.

Vol. 5 *Study Stories of Human Rights*, 3 Parts. ISBN 81-7141-607-3.

Vol. 6 *International Meetings on Human Rights*, 2 Parts. ISBN 81-7141-608-X.

Vol. 7 *Professional Training in Human Rights*. ISBN 81-7141-609-8.

Bhaskara Rao, Digumarti, Editor (2001). *Jomtein Decade of Education*. New Delhi: Discovery Publishing House. pp. 106. ISBN 81-7141-618-7.

Bhaskara Rao, Digumarti, Editor (2001). *Nuclear Materials: Issues and Concerns*, 2 Volumes. New Delhi: Discovery Publishing House. pp. 1100. ISBN 81-7141-611-X.

Bhaskara Rao, Digumarti, Editor (2001). *World Conference on Education for All*. New Delhi: APH Publishing Corporation. pp. 380. ISBN 81-7141-274-9.

Bhaskara Rao, Digumarti, Editor (2001). *World Conference on Higher Education*, New Delhi: Discovery Publishing House. pp. 306. ISBN 81-7141-610-1.

Bhaskara Rao, Digumarti, Editor (2001). *World Conference on Science*. New Delhi: Discovery Publishing House. pp. 85. ISBN 81-7141-612-8.

Bhaskara Rao, Digumarti, Editor (2004). *Chernobyl: Never Again*. New Delhi: Discovery Publishing House.

Bhaskara Rao, Digumarti, Editor (2004). *Habitat Agenda*. New Delhi: Discovery Publishing House.

Bhaskara Rao, Digumarti, Editor (2003). *Inspiring Experiences in Teacher Education*. New Delhi: Discovery Publishing House. pp. 256. ISBN 81-7141-656-X.

Bhaskara Rao, Digumarti, Editor (2003). *International Studies in Education*, 3 Volumes. New Delhi: Discovery Publishing House. pp. 912. ISBN 81-7141-647-0 (Set).

Bhaskara Rao, Digumarti, Editor (2003). *Military Conversion: Impact on Science and Technology*, New Delhi: Discovery Publishing House. pp. 200. ISBN 81-7141-578-4.

Bhaskara Rao, Digumarti, Editor (2004). *Virology and Immunology*. New Delhi: Discovery Publishing House.

Bhaskara Rao, Digumarti, Editor (2003). *United Nations Millennium Summit*. New Delhi: Discovery Publishing House. pp. 112. ISBN 81-7141-632-2.

Bhaskara Rao, Digumarti, Editor (2003). *World Assembly on Aging*. New Delhi: Discovery Publishing House. pp. 88. ISBN 81-7141-637-3.

Bhaskara Rao, Digumarti, Editor (2004). *World Conference on Human Rights*. New Delhi: Discovery Publishing House.

Bhaskara Rao, Digumarti, Editor (2003). *World Education Forum*. New Delhi: Discovery Publishing House. pp. 336. ISBN 81-7141-639-X.

Bhaskara Rao, Digumarti, Editor (2004). *Education Employment and Human Resource Development*. New Delhi: Discovery Publishing House.

Bhaskara Rao, Digumarti, Editor (2004). *Learning to Live Together*, 3 Volumes. New Delhi: Discovery Publishing House.

Bhaskara Rao, Digumarti, Editor (2004). *Successfully Schooling*. New Delhi: Discovery Publishing House.

Bhaskara Rao, Digumarti, Editor (2004). *European Education and Teachers*. New Delhi: Discovery Publishing House.

Bhaskara Rao, Digumarti, Editor (2004). *Teachers in a Changing World*. New Delhi: Discovery Publishing House.

Bhaskara Rao, Digumarti, Editor (2003). *All for Education: Sharing Strategies and Experiences in Education*. New Delhi: APH Publishing Corporation.

Bhaskara Rao, Digumarti, C.A.P. Swamy and B.S.V. Dutt (1997). *Self-Evaluation in Student Teaching*. New Delhi: Discovery Publishing House. pp. 762. ISBN 81-7141-374-9.

Bhaskara Rao, Digumarti and Digumarti Pushpa Latha (1994). *Achievement in Biology*. New Delhi: Discovery Publishing House. pp. 102. ISBN 81-7141-264-5.

Bhaskara Rao, Digumarti, C. Sridevi and K. Vijaya (1995). *Achievement in Social Studies*. New Delhi: Discovery Publishing House. pp. 102. ISBN 81-7141-281-5.

Bhaskara Rao, Digumarti and Digumarti Pushpa Latha (1995). *Achievement in English*. New Delhi: Discovery Publishing House. pp. 214. ISBN 81-7141-283-1.

Bhaskara Rao, Digumarti and Digumarti Pushpa Latha (1994). *Achievement in Science*. New Delhi: Discovery Publishing House. pp. 159. ISBN 81-7141-280-70.

Bhaskara Rao, Digumarti and Digumarti Pushpa Latha (1995). *Achievement in Mathematics*. New Delhi: Discovery Publishing House. pp. 125. ISBN 81-7141-278-5.

Bhaskara Rao, Digumarti and Digumarti Pushpa Latha, Editors (1998). *International Encyclopaedia of Women*. 5 Volumes. New Delhi: Discovery Publishing House. pp. 2172. ISBN 81-7141-410-9.

Vol. 1 *Status of World's Women*. pp. 427. ISBN 81-7141-494-X.

Vol. 2 *Women, Education and Empowerment*. pp. 467. ISBN 81-7141-498-1.

Vol. 3 *Women Challenges and Advancement*. pp. 354. ISBN 81-7141-497-4.

Vol. 4 *Women and Family Health*. pp. 470. ISBN 81-7141-497-4.

Vol. 5 *Women and International Action*. pp. 453. ISBN 81-7141-498-2.

Bhaskara Rao, Digumarti, Digumarti Pushpa Latha and Digumarti Harshitha, Editors (2001). *Biological Warfare*. New Delhi: Discovery Publishing House. pp. 422. ISBN 81-7141-597-0.

Bhaskara Rao, Digumarti, Digumarti Pushpa Latha and Digumarti Harshitha, Editors (2001). *Women as Educators*. New Delhi: Discovery Publishing House. pp. 112. ISBN 81-7141-602-0.

Bhaskara Rao, Digumarti, Digumarti Pushpa Latha and Digumarti Harshitha, Editors (2001). *Education in India*. New Delhi: APH Publishing Corporation. pp. 280. ISBN 81-7141-207-2.

Bhaskara Rao, Digumarti, Digumarti Pushpa Latha and Digumarti Harshitha, Editors (2001). *Assessing Learning Achievement*. New Delhi: Discovery Publishing House. pp. 128. ISBN 81-7141-601-2.

Bhaskara Rao, Digumarti, Digumarti Pushpa Latha and Digumarti Harshitha, Editors (2001). *Energy Security*. New Delhi: Discovery Publishing House. pp. 564. ISBN 81-7141-598-9.

Bhaskara Rao, Digumarti, Digumarti Harshitha and K.R.S.S. Rao, Editors (1999). *Advanced Biotechnology*. New Delhi: Discovery Publishing House. pp. 335. ISBN 81-7141-516-4.

Bhaskara Rao, Digumarti and D. Sridhar (2002). *Job Satisfaction of School Teachers*. New Delhi: Discovery Publishing House. pp. 104. ISBN 81-7141-652-7.

Bhaskara Rao, Digumarti and K.R.S. Sambhasiva Rao, Editors (1996). *Current Trends in Indian Education*. New Delhi: Discovery Publishing House. pp. 234. ISBN 81-7141-311-0.

Bhaskara Rao, Digumarti and K. Vijaya (1995). *A Text Book of Evaluation*. Ambala Cantt: The Associated Publishers. pp. 100.

Bhaskara Rao, Digumarti and N.V.M. Mohana Rao (2002). *Problems of Mentally Handicapped Children*. New Delhi: Discovery Publishing House. pp. 96. ISBN 81-7141-645-4.

Bhaskara Rao, Digumarti and S. Chandra Mohan (2002). *Student Participation in Sports and Games*. New Delhi: APH Publishing Corporation.

Bhaskara Rao, Digumarti, V.V. Rao, V.V. Lakshmi and V.V. Krishna, Editors (1999). *Status and Advancement of Women*. New Delhi: APH Publishing Corporation. pp. 570. ISBN 81-7648-169-6.

Babu, P.C. Author and Digumarti Bhaskara Rao, Editor (2004). *Flowers of Wisdom*. New Delhi: Discovery Publishing House.

Bhagya Lakshmi, Lingineni, Author and Digumarti Bhaskara Rao, Editor (2000). *Reading and Comprehension*. New Delhi: Discovery Publishing House. pp. 108. ISBN 81-7141-543-1.

Bhuvaneswara Lakshmi, Gadde, Author and Digumarti Bhaskara Rao, Editor (2000). *Attitude Towards Science*. New Delhi: Discovery Publishing House. pp. 128. ISBN 81-7141-541-6.

Devraj, T.A.S., Author and Digumarti Bhaskara Rao, Editor (1997). *Trace Analysis of Uranium and Thorium*. New Delhi: Discovery Publishing House. pp. 195. ISBN 81-7141-375-7.

Durga Rani, K., Author and Digumarti Bhaskara Rao, Editor (2000). *Educational Aspirations and Scientific Attitudes*. New Delhi: Discovery Publishing House. pp. 130. ISBN 81-7141-555-55.

Dutt, B.S.V. and Digumarti Bhaskara Rao (2001). *Empowering Primary Teachers*. New Delhi: Discovery Publishing House. pp. 283. ISBN 81-7141-615.2.

Ediger, Marlow and Digumarti Bhaskara Rao (1996). *Science Curriculum*. New Delhi: Discovery Publishing House. pp. 309. ISBN 81-7141-321-8.

Ediger, Marlow and Digumarti Bhaskara Rao (2000). *Teaching Mathematics Successfully*. New Delhi: Discovery Publishing House. pp. 179. ISBN 81-7141-552-0.

Ediger, Marlow and Digumarti Bhaskara Rao (2001). *Teaching Science Successfully*. New Delhi: Discovery Publishing House. pp. 320. ISBN 81-7141-600-4.

Ediger, Marlow and Digumarti Bhaskara Rao (2001). *Teaching Social Studies Successfully*. New Delhi: Discovery Publishing House. pp. 296. ISBN 81-7141-596-2.

Ediger, Marlow and Digumarti Bhaskara Rao (2002). *Philosophy and Curriculum*. New Delhi: Discovery Publishing House. pp. 224. ISBN 81-7141-631-4.

Ediger, Marlow and Digumarti Bhaskara Rao (2002). *Improving School Administration*. New Delhi: Discovery Publishing House. pp. 240. ISBN 81-7141-633-0.

Ediger, Marlow and Digumarti Bhaskara Rao (2002). *Elementary Curriculum*. New Delhi: Discovery Publishing House. pp. 490. ISBN 81-7141-658-6.

Ediger, Marlow and Digumarti Bhaskara Rao (2003). *Language Arts Curriculum*. New Delhi: Discovery Publishing House. pp. 348. ISBN 81-7141-657-8.

Ediger, Marlow and Digumarti Bhaskara Rao (2001). *The Holy Land*. New Delhi: Discovery Publishing House.

Ediger, Marlow and Digumarti Bhaskara Rao (2004). *Psychology and Curriculum*. New Delhi: Discovery Publishing House.

Ediger, Marlow and Digumarti Bhaskara Rao (2004). *Teaching Language Arts Successfully*. New Delhi: Discovery Publishing House.

Ediger, Marlow and Digumarti Bhaskara Rao (2004). *Psychology and Curriculum*. New Delhi: Discovery Publishing House.

Ediger, Marlow and Digumarti Bhaskara Rao (2004). *Teaching Mathematics in Elementary Schools*. New Delhi: Discovery Publishing House.

Ediger, Marlow and Digumarti Bhaskara Rao (2004). *Teaching Science in Elementary Schools*. New Delhi: Discovery Publishing House.

Ediger, Marlow and Digumarti Bhaskara Rao (2004). *Teaching Social Studies in Elementary Schools*. New Delhi: Discovery Publishing House.

Ediger, Marlow and Digumarti Bhaskara Rao (2004). *School Curriculum and Administration*. New Delhi: Discovery Publishing House.

Ediger, Marlow and Digumarti Bhaskara Rao (2004): *Relevancy in Elementary Curriculum*. New Delhi: Discovery Publishing House.

Ediger, Marlow and Digumarti Bhaskara Rao (2004). *Elementary Curriculum Improvement*. New Delhi: Discovery Publishing House.

Ediger Marlow, B.S.V. Dutt and Digumarti Bhaskara Rao (2004). *Teaching English Successfully*. New Delhi: Discovery Publishing House.

Jayasree, Kandi, Author and Digumarti Bhaskara Rao, Editor (1999). *Correlates of Socialisation*. New Delhi: Discovery Publishing House. pp. 160. ISBN 81-7141-517-2.

John Babu, Chikati, Author and T.J.R. Prasad, G.M. Madhukar and Digumarti Bhaskara Rao, Editors (1996). *Problem Solving in Mathematics*. New Delhi: APH Publishing Corporation. pp. 125. ISBN 81-7648-273-0.

Jyothi, Nirmala M., Author and Digumarti Bhaskara Rao, Editor (2003). *Non-Detention System in School Education*. New Delhi: Discovery Publishing House. pp. 400. ISBN 81-7141-654-3.

Marja, Talvi and Digumarti Bhaskara Rao, Editors (1996). *Educational Leadership and Social Changes*. New Delhi: Discovery Publishing House. pp. 236. ISBN 81-7141-320-X.

Prabhakaram, K.S., Author and Digumarti Bhaskara Rao, Editor (1998). *Concept Attainment Model in Mathematics Teaching*. New Delhi: Discovery Publishing House. pp. 122. ISBN 81-7141-424-9.

Prasanth Kumar, J., Author and Digumarti Bhaskara Rao, Editor (1998). *Effectiveness of Distance Education System*. New Delhi: Discovery Publishing House. pp. 152. ISBN 81-7141-437-0.

Ramatulasamma, K., Author and Digumarti Bhaskara Rao, Editor (2002). *Job Satisfaction of Teacher Educators*, New Delhi: Discovery Publishing House. pp. 160. ISBN 81-7141-655-1.

Rama Krishnaiah, D., Author and Digumarti Bhaskara Rao, Editor (1998). *Job Satisfaction of College Teachers*, New Delhi: Discovery Publishing House. pp. 251. ISBN 81-7141-438-9.

Rathaiah, Lavu and Digumarti Bhaskara Rao, Editors (1996). *International Innovations in Education*. New Delhi: Discovery Publishing House. pp. 513. ISBN 81-7141-359-5.

Ramesh, Ganta and Digumarti Bhaskara Rao, Editors (1998). *Environmental Education: Problems and Prospects*. New Delhi: Discovery Publishing House. pp. 324. ISBN 81-7141-423-0.

Rathaiah, Lavu and Digumarti Bhaskara Rao (1997). *Achievement Correlates*. New Delhi: Discovery Publishing House. pp. 116. ISBN 81-7141-385-4.

Reddy, Sudhakar Y., Author, and Digumarti Bhaskara Rao, Editor (2003). *Creativity in Adolescents*. New Delhi: Discovery Publishing House. pp. 430. ISBN 81-7141-659-4.

Reddy, M.S., Author and Digumarti Bhaskara Rao, Editor (2004). *Creativity in College Students*. New Delhi: Discovery Publishing House.

Radramamba, B., Author and Digumarti Bhaskara Rao, Editor (2003). *Problems of Teaching*. New Delhi: APH Publishing Corporation. pp. 203. ISBN 81-7648-462-8.

Sanjeeva Rao, P.C., Author and Digumarti Bhaskara Rao, Editor (1996). *A Text Book of Geology*. New Delhi: Discovery Publishing House. pp. 320. ISBN 81-7141-313-7.

Satya Narayana V., Author and Digumarti Bhaskara Rao, Editor (2001). *Physical Education, Social Attitudes and Leadership Qualities*. New Delhi: Discovery Publishing House. pp. 296. ISBN 81-7141-593-8.

Srinivasulu Reddy, M., and K.R.S. Sambasiva Rao, Authors and Digumarti Bhaskara Rao, Editor (1999). *A Text Book of Aquaculture*. New Delhi: Discovery Publishing House. pp. 296. ISBN 81-7141-482-6.

Srinivasa Rao, Mandalapu, Author and Digumarti Bhaskara Rao, Editor (2004). *Achievement Motivation and Achievement in Mathematics*. New Delhi: Discovery Publishing House.

Valeri V. Koustiouk, Author and Digumarti Bhaskara Rao, Editor (2002). *A Text Book of Cryogenics*. New Delhi: Discovery Publishing House. pp. 288. ISBN 81-7141-642-X.

Valeri V. Koustiouk, Author and Digumarti Bhaskara Rao, Editor (2004). *Refrigeration and Environment*. New Delhi: Discovery Publishing House.

Vanaja, M., Author and Digumarti Bhaskara Rao, Editor (1999). *Inquiry Training Model*. New Delhi: Discovery Publishing House. pp. 189. ISBN 81-7141-515-6.

Veena Kumari, Balusu and Digumarti Bhaskara Rao (1996). *Operation Black Board*. New Delhi: Ashish Publishing Corporation. pp. 140. ISBN 81-7024-711-X.

Veena Kumari, Balusu, Author and Digumarti Bhaskara Rao, Editor (2000). *Psycho-Social Correlates of Achievement*, New Delhi: Discovery Publishing House. pp. 36. ISBN 81-7141-547-4.

Venkata Rao, P. and Digumarti Bhaskara Rao (1989). *A Text Book of Zoology—Junior Intermediate*. Guntur: Vignan Publishers. pp. 370.

Venkata Rao, P. and Digumarti Bhaskara Rao (1989). *A Text Book of Zoology—Senior Intermediate*. Guntur: Vignan Publishers. pp. 480.

Venugopala Rao, K., Author and Digumarti Bhaskara Rao, Editor (2000). *Teacher Morale in Secondary Schools*. New Delhi: Discovery Publishing House. pp. 300. ISBN 81-7141-551-2.

Vidya, C., Author and Digumarti Bhaskara Rao. Editor (1996). *A Text Book of Nutrition*. New Delhi: Discovery Publishing House. pp. 438. ISBN 81-7141-309-9.

Vidya Bharathi, D., Author and Digumarti Bhaskara Rao, Editor (2000). *Educational Philosophies of Swami Vivekananda and John Dewey*. New Delhi: APH Publishing Corporation. pp. 200. ISBN 81-7648-309-9.

Books in Telugu Language

Bhaskara Rao, Digumarti (1986). *Dhrushya Sravana Bodhanapakaranalu* (Audio Visual Teaching Aids). Guntur: Nagarjuna Publishers.

Bhaskara Rao, Digumarti (1993). *Jeevasashtra Bodhana* (Teaching of Biology). Guntur: Nagarjuna Publishers.

Bhaskara Rao, Digumarti (1995). *Vignanasasthra Bodhana* (Teaching of Science) Guntur: Nagarjuna Publishers.

Bhaskara Rao, Digumarti (1997). *Vidya Manovignana Seshtram* (Educational Psychology). Guntur: Creative Press. pp. 434. Rs. 79.

Bhaskara Rao, Digumarti (1998). *DSC Study Material*. Guntur: Nagarjuna Publishers.

Bhaskara Rao, Digumarti (1998). *Upadhyayudu Vidya*. (Teacher and Education). Guntur: Nagarjuna Publishers.

Bhaskara Rao, Digumarti (1998). *Vidya Drukpadalu* (Prespectives of Education). Guntur: Nagarjuna Publishers.

Bhaskara Rao, Digumarti (1999). *EdCET Teaching Aptitude*. Guntur: Nagarjuna Publishers.

Bhaskara Rao, Digumarti (2001). *Bharata Samajamulo Upadyayudu Vidya* (Teacher and Education in Emerging Indian Society). Guntur: Nagarjuna Publishers.

Bhaskara Rao, Digumarti (2001). *Bhoutika Sastra Bodhana Paddathulu* (Methods of Teaching Physical Science). Guntur: Nagarjuna Publishers. pp. 324.

Bhaskara Rao, Digumarti (2001). *Jeeva Sastra Bodhana Padhathulu* (Methods of Teaching Biology). Guntur: Nagarjuna Publishers. pp. 224.

Bhaskara Rao, Digumarti (2001). *Vidya Manovignana Sastram* (Educational Psychology). Guntur: Nagarjuna Publishers. pp. 344.

Bhaskara Rao, Digumarti (2003). *Patsala Yajamanyam / Paripalana* (School Management and Administration). Guntur: Nagarjuna Publishers.

Bhaskara Rao, Digumarti (2004). *Vidya Sanketika Sastram mariyu Computer Vidya* (Educational Technology and Computer Education). Guntur: Nagarjuna Publishers.

APPENDIX—A

EDUCATIONAL LIBERALISM-CONSERVATISM SCALE

I. Aims of Education

1. Education is a process of life.
2. Salvation of one's soul is the ultimate goal of all educational activities.
3. Only pupils with superior intellectual ability should be permitted for higher education.
4. The pupil's social adjustment, emotional development, physical well-being and vocational competence should also be emphasized as aims of education along with the development of the intellect.
5. Education should make the human being understand aim of creation.
6. Youth's natural tendencies should be developed to their fullest through education.
7. True education is based upon the needs, interests and natural desires of the child.
8. Development of the intellect of the child alone is the main aim of education.

II. Purpose of the School

9. The development of the whole child is the main purpose of the school.

10. There are no ultimate goals of the school.
11. Physical development is outside the realm of school education.
12. All educational activities should aim at the means of perfecting the intellect of the child.
13. The school should develop in each pupil a proper attitude towards obedience to authority.
14. The school should be organised as a miniature society.

III. Curriculum

15. Only experts or scholars should determine the curriculum content.
16. Curriculum is defined in terms of what a student does rather than what he is taught.
17. Certain constant principles should determine the important content of education.
18. Physical and vocational education should be given prominent place in the curriculum.
19. The formal curriculum in schools should be essentially the same for all.
20. Utility should be the first criterion for selection of curricular offerings.
21. The study of the political and social structures under which the pupils are living should be emphasized in the curriculum.
22. Religion should be given a principal place in the curriculum.
23. All activities which take place under the direction and control of the school one integral elements of curriculum.
24. Only subjects and activities which perfect the intellect of the child should be included in the curriculum.
25. A wide range of subjects and activities must be offered to satisfy student interests.
26. Curriculum should be close to life.

IV. Methodology

27. The pupil can learn any subject through observation of nature not by reading books or being told about it.
28. Whenever possible, the student must learn from first hand experience.
29. Teacher's convenience, not of the child, is the criterion of any method.
30. The teacher should utilise the pupil's natural desire for play in teaching-learning process.
31. Only the teacher should be the active agent during the class period.
32. The pupils are the actors, the teacher is the co-ordinator of the various acts.
33. It is possible to adjust our teaching to suit the individual differences among pupils.
34. Lecture method is the best means of transmitting knowledge to the students.
35. Recitation is the major means of determining the student's mastery over the material presented to her/him in Indian conditions.
36. The teacher is to assist students to discover knowledge.
37. Project method should receive primary attention in teaching.
38. Only deductive reasoning should be developed in pupils.
39. Problem solving methods can find a place in Indian schools.
40. Reason alone is the primary mode of knowing.

V. Freedom and Discipline

41. Strict discipline in schools results in the development of disciplined citizens.
42. Use of corporal punishment should be discouraged.
43. The laws of good social living are to be lived in the school rather than taught there.

44. No one should question about the disciplinary measures used by the school.

45. Discipline is a social process involving every person in the group.

46. The teacher should have absolute control over his pupils.

47. Punishment will never change the pupil.

48. In achieving the intellectual discipline, rigid form of classroom discipline is a necessary means.

49. The discipline problem of the student will vanish if the environment is corrected.

50. The native instincts and desires of children should be constantly held in check.

VI. Evaluation

51. Mastery over the prescribed subject matter of a particular grade is the criterion for promotion.

52. The primary objective of evaluation is "to assess a pupil's growth in all phases of living" rather than "the mastery of subject matter by a child."

53. The practice of non-detention should be discarded.

54. Pupil's self-evaluation is more important than that of the teacher or outside authorities.

55. A variety of techniques, beside essay and oral examinations, to test the applicative abilities should be intensively used in evaluating the pupils.

56. Only an essay or oral examination will provide the opportunity for the student to display the different mental abilities.

APPENDIX—B

PURPOSE IN LIFE (P.I.L.) SCALE

Instructions

For each of the following statements, circle the number that would be most nearly true for you. Note that the numbers always extend from one extreme feeling to its opposite kind of feeling. Neutral implies no judgement either way. Try to use this rating as little as possible.

1 (-Negative)	and	7 (+Positive)	Completely/always/exactly/very/no utterly and so on.
2	and	6	Mostly/frequently/to a great extent and so on.
3	and	5	Sometimes/Occasionally/to some extent.
4			Neutral

1. I am usually:

1	2	3	4	5	6	7
completely bored			Neutral			exuberent enthusiastic

2. Life to me seems:

7	6	5	4	3	2	1
always exciting			Neutral			completely routine

3. In life I have:

1	2	3	4	5	6	7
no goals or aims at all			neutral			very clear goals and aims

4. My personal existence is:

1	2	3	4	5	6	7
utterly meaning-less and without purpose			neutral			very purposeful and meaningful

(Contd...)

5. Every day is:

7	6	5	4	3	2	1
constantly new			Neutral			exactly the same

6. If I could choose, I would:

1	2	3	4	5	6	7
prefer never to have been born			Neutral			like 9 more lives just like this one

7. After retiring I would:

7	6	5	4	3	2	1
do some of the exciting things I have always wanted to			Neutral			take complete rest in my life

8. In achieving life goals, I have:

1	2	3	4	5	6	7
made no progress whatever			Neutral			progressed to complete fulfilment

9. My life is:

1	2	3	4	5	6	7
empty and filled only with despair			Neutral			thrilling, running over with exciting good things

10. If I should die today, I would feel that my life has been:

7	6	5	4	3	2	1
very worthwhile			Neutral			completely worthless

11. In thinking of my life I:

1	2	3	4	5	6	7
often wonder why I exist?			Neutral			always see a reason for my being here

12. As I view the world in relation to my life, the world:

1	2	3	4	5	6	7
completely confuses me			Neutral			fits meaningfully with my life

(Contd...)

13. I am a:

1	2	3	4	5	6	7
very irresponsible person			Neutral			very responsible person

14. Concerning man's freedom to make his own choices,. I believe man is:

7	6	5	4	3	2	1
absolutely free to make all life choices			Neutral			completely bound by limitation of heredity and environment

15. With regard to death, I am:

7	6	5	4	3	2	1
prepared and unafraid			Neutral			unprepared and frightened

16. With regard to suicide, I have:

1	2	3	4	5	6	7
thought of it seriously as is way out			Neutral			never given it a second thought

17. I regard my ability to find a meaning, purpose or mission in life as:

7	6	5	4	3	2	1
very great			Neutral			practically none

18. My life is:

7	6	5	4	3	2	1
in my hands and I am in control of it			Neutral			out of my hands and controlled by external factors

19. Facing my daily tasks is:

7	6	5	4	3	2	1
a source of pleasure and satisfaction			Neutral			a painful and boring experience

20. I have discovered:

1	2	3	4	5	6	7
no mission or purpose in life			Neutral			clearcut goals and a satisfying life purpose

APPENDIX—C

RESPONSE SHEET

1. Name of the teacher trainee :
2. Name of the college of education :
3. Sex : Male/Female
4. First methodology subject : Maths/Physical sciences
   Biological sciences/
   social studies

A: E.L.C.S.

Item No.	A	D	*Item No.*	A	D	*Item No.*	A	D	*Item No.*	A	D
1			15.			29.			43.		
2.			16.			30.			44.		
3.			17.			31.			45.		
4.			18.			32.			46.		
5.			19.			33.			47.		
6.			20.			34.			48.		
7.			21.			35.			49.		
8.			22.			36.			50.		
9.			23.			37.			51.		
10.			24.			38.			52.		
11.			25.			39.			53.		
12.			26.			40.			54.		
13.			27.			41.			55.		
14.			28.			42.			56.		

B. P.I.L.

Item No.	*Position on the scale*	*Item No.*	*Position on the scale*
1.		11.	
2.		12.	
3.		13.	
4.		14.	
5.		15.	
6.		16.	
7.		17.	
8.		18.	
9.		19.	
10.		20.	

Index